AQA STUDY GUIDE

GCSE 9–1

THE STRANGE CASE OF
DR JEKYLL & MR HYDE

BY ROBERT LOUIS STEVENSON

REVISION & PRACTICE
ALL IN ONE BOOK

SCHOLASTIC

Author Marie Lallaway

Series Consultants Richard Durant and Cindy Torn

Reviewer Rob Pollard

Editorial team Rachel Morgan, Audrey Stokes, Camilla Erskine, Lesley Densham, Anne Henwood, Louise Titley

Typesetting Oxford Designers and Illustrators

Cover design Nicolle Thomas and Neil Salt

App development Hannah Barnett, Phil Crothers and Haremi Ltd

Acknowledgements

Illustration Jim Eldridge/Oxford Designers & Illustrators

Photographs pages 14 and 58: Hyde silhouette, Dave scar/ Shutterstock; page 16: Robert Louis Stevenson, duncan1890/ istock; page 17: Big Ben, jeafish Ping/Shutterstock; pages 18 and 82: magnifying glass, Yulia Glam/Shutterstock; pages 23 and 27: ink and quill, Kozini/Shutterstock; pages 34 and 73: London street, Unholy Vault Designs/Shutterstock; page 42: decanter and glass, Oleg Zorchenko/Shutterstock; page 46: key, Africa Studio/Shutterstock; page 48: axe, Volodymyr Nikitenko/Shutterstock; page 53: Adam and Eve, Zvonimir Atletic/Shutterstock; page 54: gothic hand, Forgem/Shutterstock; pages 60 and 71: Charles Darwin, Everett Historical/Shutterstock; page 68: Queen Victoria, Everett Historical/Shutterstock; page 69: Burke and Hare, Colport/Alamy Stock Photo; page 70: Sigmund Freud, Everett Historical/Shutterstock; page 74: censored graphic, Bankrx/Shutterstock; page 76: street lights, Tony Craddock/ Shutterstock; page 78: pocket watch, Neirfy/Shutterstock; page 90: girl doing exam, Monkey Business Images/ Shutterstock; page 93: notepad and pen, TRINACRIA PHOTO/Shutterstock

Designed using Adobe InDesign

Published by Scholastic Education, an imprint of Scholastic Ltd, Book End, Range Road, Witney, Oxfordshire, OX29 0YD
Registered office: Westfield Road, Southam, Warwickshire CV47 0RA
www.scholastic.co.uk

Printed by Bell and Bain
© 2019 Scholastic Ltd
1 2 3 4 5 6 7 8 9 9 0 1 2 3 4 5 6 7 8

British Library Cataloguing-in-Publication Data
A catalogue record for this book is available from the British Library.

ISBN 978-1407-18264-3

Note from the publisher:
Please use this product in conjunction with the official specification and sample assessment materials. Ask your teacher if you are unsure where to find them.

Contents

**Check your answers on
the free revision app or at
www.scholastic.co.uk/gcse**

How to use this book

This Study Guide is designed to help you prepare effectively for your AQA GCSE English literature exam question on *The Strange Case of Dr Jekyll and Mr Hyde* (Paper 1, Section B).

The content has been organised in a sequence that builds confidence, and which will deepen your knowledge and understanding of the novel step by step. Therefore, it is best to work through this book in the order that it is presented.

This Study Guide uses the Scholastic Classics edition.

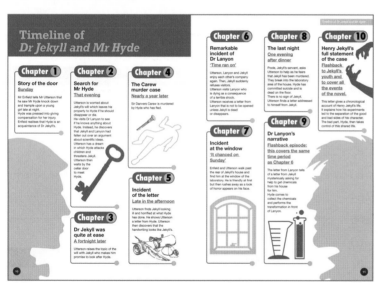

Know the plot

1 It is very important that you know the plot well: to be clear about what happens and in what order. The **timeline** on pages 10–11 provides a useful overview of the plot, highlighting key events.

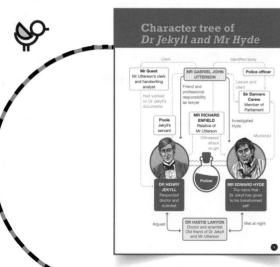

The **character tree** on page 9 introduces you to the main characters of the text.

The chronological section

2 The chronological section on pages 12–61 takes you through the novel chapter by chapter, providing plot summaries and pointing out important details. It is also designed to help you think about the structure of the novel.

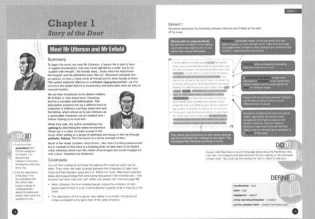

This section provides an in-depth exploration of themes or character development, drawing your attention to how Stevenson's language choices reveal the novel's meaning.

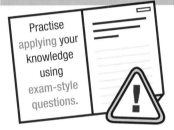

Practise applying your knowledge using exam-style questions.

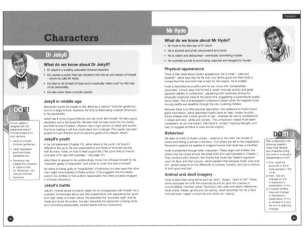

The novel as a whole

3 The second half of the guide is retrospective: it helps you to look back over the whole novel through a number of relevant 'lenses': characters, themes, Stevenson's language, form and structural features.

Doing well in your AQA Exam

Stick to the **TIME LIMITS** you will need to in the exam.

4 Finally, you will find an extended 'Doing well in your AQA exam' section which guides you through the process of understanding questions, and planning and writing answers.

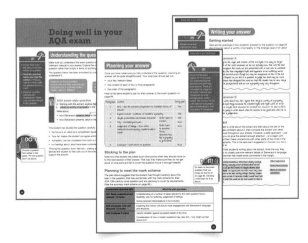

Features of this guide

The best way to retain information is to take an active approach to revision.

Throughout this book, you will find lots of features that will make your revision an active, successful process.

SNAPIT!

Use the Snap it! feature in the revision app to take pictures of key concepts and information. Great for revision on the go!

DEFINEIT!

Explains the meaning of difficult words from the set texts.

Callouts Additional explanations of important points.

words shown in **purple bold** can be found in the glossary on pages 94–95

Find methods of relaxation that work for you throughout the revision period.

Regular exercise helps stimulate the brain and will help you relax.

DOIT!

Activities to embed your knowledge and understanding and prepare you for the exams.

NAILIT!

Succinct and vital tips on how to do well in your exam.

STRETCHIT!

Provides content that stretches you further.

REVIEW IT!

Helps you to consolidate and understand what you have learned before moving on.

Revise in pairs or small groups and deliver presentations on topics to each other.

FOR HIGH-MARK QUESTIONS, SPEND TIME **PLANNING** YOUR ANSWER!

AQA exam-style question

AQA exam-style sample questions based on the extract shown are given on some pages. Use the sample mark scheme on page 86 to help you assess your responses. This will also help you understand what you could do to improve your response.

FREE REVISION APP

- The **free revision app** can be downloaded to your mobile phone (iOS and Android), making **on the go revision** easy.

- Use the revision calendar to help map out your revision in the lead-up to the exam.

- Complete multiple-choice questions and create your own SNAP revision cards.

www.scholastic.co.uk/gcse

Online answers and additional resources
All of the tasks in this book are designed to get you thinking and to consolidate your understanding through thought and application. Therefore, it is important to write your own answers before checking. Some questions include tables where you need to fill in your answer in the book. Other questions require you to use a separate piece of paper so that you can draft your response and work out the best way of answering.

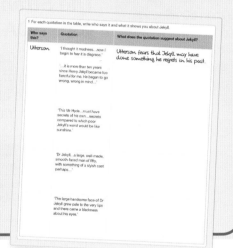

Get plenty of sleep, especially the night before an exam.

⚠ **LOOK AFTER YOURSELF**

Help your brain by looking after your whole body!

Once you have worked through a section, you can check your answers to Do it!, Stretch it!, Review it! and the exam practice sections on the app or at **www.scholastic.co.uk/gcse**.

Why study *The Strange Case of Dr Jekyll and Mr Hyde*?

Even before you read *The Strange Case of Dr Jekyll and Mr Hyde*, you may have heard the names of the two characters in the title.

The novel was extremely popular when it was published in 1886. The Victorian readership would have been intrigued, shocked, startled and horrified as events unfold. Stevenson's language may at first be unfamiliar to a modern reader but if you persevere, you will soon find yourself able to enjoy the central ideas of hidden lives, supernatural events, crime, violence and death.

The Strange Case of Dr Jekyll and Mr Hyde in your AQA exam

The Strange Case of Dr Jekyll and Mr Hyde is examined in Section B (the second half) of the first AQA GCSE English Literature exam, Paper 1: Shakespeare and 19th-century novel. Here is how it fits into the overall assessment framework:

Paper 1 Time: **1 hour 45 minutes**	Paper 2 Time: **2 hours 15 minutes**
Section A: Shakespeare	Section A: Modern prose or drama
Section B: 19th-century novel: *The Strange Case of Dr Jekyll and Mr Hyde*	Section B: Poetry anthology
	Section C: Unseen poetry

There will be just one question on *The Strange Case of Dr Jekyll and Mr Hyde* and you should not answer questions on any other 19th-century novel. Just answer the *The Strange Case of Dr Jekyll and Mr Hyde* question. You should spend 50 minutes planning and writing your answer to the question. There are 30 marks available for the 19th-century novel question.

The 19th-century novel question will come with a short extract from the novel printed on the exam paper. You will find the question straight after the extract. The question will focus on character and/or theme. You must answer the question in relation to the extract and to relevant other parts of the novel that you have chosen.

A character tree

The 'character tree' on page 9 should help you to fix in your mind the names of the characters, their relationships and who did what to whom.

Timeline of *The Strange Case of Dr Jekyll and Mr Hyde*

The timeline on pages 10–11 provides a visual overview of the plot, highlighting key events which take place over the course of the novel. It will also help you to think about the structure of the novel.

NAILIT!

- Keep a close watch on the time in the exam. If you have chosen to answer the question on *The Strange Case of Dr Jekyll and Mr Hyde* first, don't spend more than 50 minutes on it or you will have less time to write your answer to the Shakespeare question.

Character tree of *Dr Jekyll and Mr Hyde*

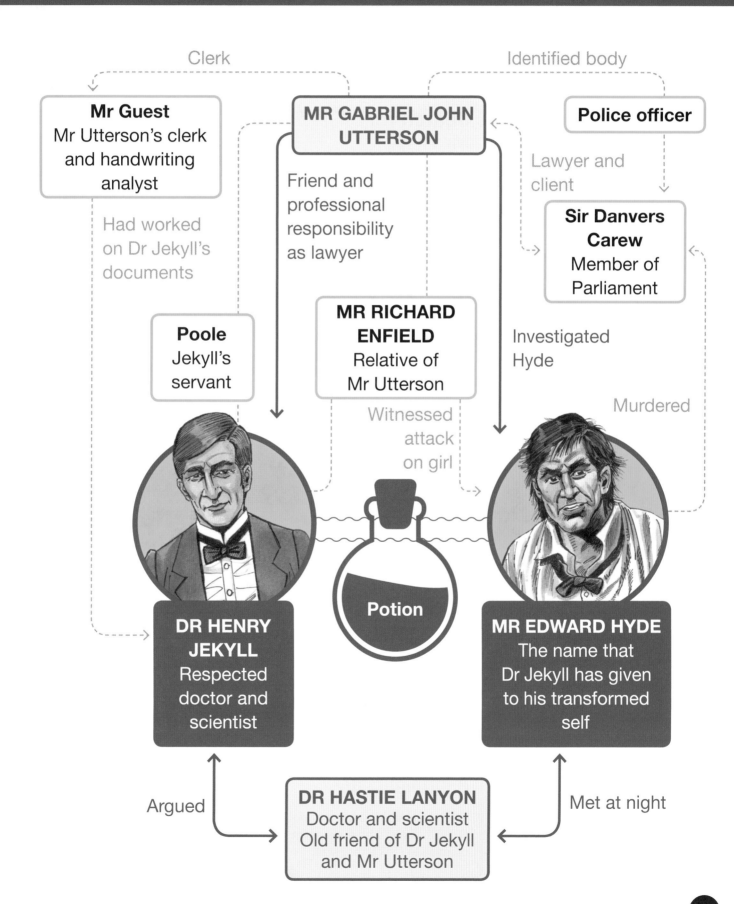

Clerk

Identified body

Mr Guest
Mr Utterson's clerk and handwriting analyst

MR GABRIEL JOHN UTTERSON

Police officer

Had worked on Dr Jekyll's documents

Friend and professional responsibility as lawyer

Lawyer and client

Sir Danvers Carew
Member of Parliament

Poole
Jekyll's servant

MR RICHARD ENFIELD
Relative of Mr Utterson

Investigated Hyde

Murdered

Witnessed attack on girl

Potion

DR HENRY JEKYLL
Respected doctor and scientist

MR EDWARD HYDE
The name that Dr Jekyll has given to his transformed self

Argued

DR HASTIE LANYON
Doctor and scientist
Old friend of Dr Jekyll and Mr Utterson

Met at night

Timeline of *Dr Jekyll and Mr Hyde*

Chapter 1

Story of the door
Sunday

Mr Enfield tells Mr Utterson that he saw Mr Hyde knock down and trample upon a young girl late at night.
Hyde was pressed into giving compensation for her injury. Enfield realises that Hyde is an acquaintance of Dr Jekyll's.

Chapter 2

Search for Mr Hyde
That evening

Utterson is worried about Jekyll's will which leaves his property to Hyde if he should disappear or die.
He visits Dr Lanyon to see if he knows anything about Hyde. Instead, he discovers that Jekyll and Lanyon had fallen out over an argument about scientific ideas.
Utterson has a dream in which Hyde attacks children and threatens Jekyll.
Utterson then waits by the cellar door to meet Hyde.

Chapter 3

Dr Jekyll was quite at ease
A fortnight later

Utterson raises the topic of the will with Jekyll who makes him promise to look after Hyde.

Chapter 4

The Carew murder case
Nearly a year later

Sir Danvers Carew is murdered by Hyde who has fled.

Chapter 5

Incident of the letter
Late in the afternoon

Utterson finds Jekyll looking ill and horrified at what Hyde has done. He shows Utterson a letter from Hyde. Utterson then discovers that the handwriting looks like Jekyll's.

Chapter 6

Remarkable incident of Dr Lanyon

'Time ran on'

Utterson, Lanyon and Jekyll enjoy each other's company again. Then, Jekyll suddenly refuses visitors.
Utterson visits Lanyon who is dying as a consequence of a terrible shock.
Utterson receives a letter from Lanyon that is not to be opened unless Jekyll is dead or disappears.

Chapter 7

Incident at the window

'It chanced on Sunday'

Enfield and Utterson walk past the rear of Jekyll's house and find him at the window of the laboratory. He is friendly at first but then rushes away as a look of horror appears on his face.

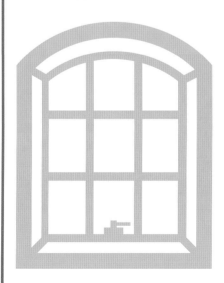

Chapter 8

The last night

One evening after dinner

Poole, Jekyll's servant, asks Utterson to help as he fears that Jekyll has been murdered. They break into the laboratory area of the house. Hyde has committed suicide and is dead on the floor.
There is no sign of Jekyll. Utterson finds a letter addressed to himself from Jekyll.

Chapter 9

Dr Lanyon's narrative

Flashback episode: this covers the same time period as Chapter 6

The letter from Lanyon tells of a letter from Jekyll mysteriously asking for help to get chemicals from his house for him.
Hyde comes to collect the chemicals and performs the transformation in front of Lanyon.

Chapter 10

Henry Jekyll's full statement of the case

Flashback to Jekyll's youth and to cover all the events of the novel.

This letter gives a chronological account of Henry Jekyll's life. It explains how his experiments led to the separation of the good and bad sides of his character. The bad part, Hyde, then takes control of this shared life.

Chapter 1
Story of the Door

Meet Mr Utterson and Mr Enfield

Summary

To begin the novel, we meet Mr Utterson, a lawyer. He is said to have 'a rugged countenance, that was never lighted by a smile' and to be 'austere with himself'; 'his friends were…those whom he had known the longest' and his affections were 'like ivy'. Stevenson presents him as serious, to have a close circle of friends and to show loyalty to them. (The author presents Utterson in a detailed **character** portrait – as if to convince the reader that he is trustworthy and believable when he tells of unusual events.)

We are then introduced to his distant relative, Mr Enfield, a 'man about town' (meaning that he is sociable and fashionable). This description presents him as a different kind of character to Utterson, but they share time and friendship, which allows us to see Utterson as a personable character, not an isolated one – further helping us to trust him.

While they walk, the author establishes the **setting** by describing the street environment. (There are a number of street scenes in the novel, often adding to a sense of darkness and decay in the city through **pathetic fallacy**. This first scene is a prime example of this.)

Much of the street contains 'shop fronts…like rows of smiling saleswomen' but in contrast to this there is a building (that we later learn to be Hyde's cellar entrance) which had 'the marks of prolonged and sordid negligence' with a door 'blistered and distained'.

Contrasts

You will find a series of contrasts throughout this novel so watch out for them. They mirror the main contrast between the characters of Jekyll and Hyde and that between good and evil. Within the novel, Stevenson explores ideas about psychology that were being discussed in the Victorian era – that humans had more than one 'self' within one person (for more see page 68).

- Here, Utterson, the level-headed lawyer, enjoys the company of man-about-town Enfield. It is as if one character supplies what is missing in the other.

- The description of the locations also refers to contrasts: the attractive shops compared to the grim door of the cellar entrance.

DO IT!

1 Find two more **quotations** from the first paragraph of Chapter 1 to demonstrate Utterson's character and explore what they show you.

2 Find the description of the door. Find two examples that the author uses to give a sense of unpleasantness about this place and explain what each one suggests to you.

Extract 1

Stevenson describes the friendship between Utterson and Enfield at the start of the novel.

Utterson did not judge his friends: this sets the foundation for his helping Jekyll rather than rejecting him for his uneven and unusual behaviours.

Metaphor: Stevenson means 'of his own family' but 'own blood' suggests a much stronger bond. Theirs is an automatic, non-judgemental, friendship which springs from a sense of duty to family – obeying social conventions.

"
It is the mark of a modest man to accept his friendly circle ready-made from the hands of opportunity; and that was the lawyer's way. His friends were those of his own blood or those whom he had known the longest;
5 his affections, like ivy, were the growth of time, they implied no aptness in the object. Hence, no doubt, the bond that united him to Mr Richard Enfield, his distant kinsman, the well-known man about town. It was a nut to crack for many, what these two could see in each
10 other, or what subject they could find in common. It was reported by those who encountered them in their Sunday walks, that they said nothing, looked singularly dull, and would hail with obvious relief the appearance of a friend. For all that, the two men put
15 the greatest store by these excursions, counted them the chief jewel of each week, and not only set aside occasions of pleasure, but even resisted the calls of business, that they might enjoy them uninterrupted.
"

Similes: what is implied by comparing Utterson's friendship to ivy?

A **colloquial metaphor** is used here. Stevenson's **language** is very formal for a modern reader, but this would lighten the **tone** for Victorian reader.

People find the friendship between Utterson and Enfield puzzling as they are such different kinds of people.

Stevenson introduces the idea that people 'watch' each other. As social animals, humans are often keen to observe one another. However, Victorian codes of behaviour were much more defined than today's may be: having a good reputation is a **theme** of the novel.

They placed great importance on their regular meetings and never cancelled their meetings for any reason. This emphasises their friendship and liking of routine.

DO IT!

Explain what Stevenson's choice of language shows about the friendship of the two men in the metaphor that describes their Sunday meeting as 'the chief jewel of each week'. (You could use the example for 'like ivy' above to help you.)

DEFINE IT!

countenance – face

mark – sign

negligence – neglect

of his own blood/kinsman – a relative

put the greatest store – placed importance upon

'A very odd story'

Summary

Upon seeing the door, Mr Enfield recounts 'a very odd story'. In the early morning, he witnessed 'a little man stumping along' and 'a girl…running as hard as she was able'. They collided and the man 'trampled calmly over the child's body and left her screaming on the ground'. Enfield says that although it doesn't sound such an important event, 'it was hellish to see'. He describes how he chased the man and brought him back to the child, who was surrounded by a crowd. A doctor (who the girl had been sent to fetch) then arrived.

Through Enfield, the author describes the doctor – he had 'a strong Edinburgh accent' and was 'as emotional as a bagpipe' – and his reaction to the man; he saw the doctor 'turn sick and white with desire to kill him'. The crowd form 'a circle of…hateful faces' but the man has a 'black sneering coolness'. (These reactions may seem exaggerated to us but we later find that Hyde causes this reaction in all 'good' people. It is a first clue, especially to a Victorian reader who would be used to this convention of 'extreme emotional reaction' as part of the **Gothic literature** genre, see page 54.)

Enfield then tells how he forced the man to offer compensation. The man goes to the door and returns with a cheque in Jekyll's name. Utterson asks questions, but Enfield does not wish to talk about it, saying that he doesn't believe in asking questions, especially when there is something suspicious involved. Utterson and he agree not to talk further about this matter. (Enfield's words sum up what happens in the whole novel: 'You start a question, and it's like starting a stone' rolling that causes destruction in its path. However, Utterson's questions uncover rather than cause the destruction.)

NAIL IT

You will not have the text with you in the exam, so having a precise knowledge of pivotal parts of the novel will be essential.

This event about the child is important: it is the first of Hyde's violent acts that the reader knows about; it allows Hyde's increased level of violence to be measured – for example, he progresses from this to murder.

Create a timeline of the events in Mr Enfield's recount. Add one useful quotation to each point. This will help you to remember it clearly for use in your essays.

Explain how the language of this description is important to the novel as a whole. Focus in on words and phrases. For example:
'a little man…stumping along' – Hyde's movements are all described using **verbs** with negative **connotations**. Aggression and ill-temper are suggested in this choice of 'stumping'.

Extract 1

In this chapter, we have the first descriptions of Mr Hyde, although he is not named at this point, presented from the points of view of other characters.

> But the doctor's case was what struck me. He was the usual cut-and-dry apothecary, of no particular age and colour, with a strong Edinburgh accent, and about as emotional as a bagpipe…every time he
> 5 looked at my prisoner, I saw that Sawbones turn sick and white with the desire to kill him. I knew what was in his mind, just as he knew what was in mine; and killing being out of the question, we did the next best. We told the man we…would make such a scandal out
> 10 of this as should make his name stink…If he had any friends or any credit, we undertook that he should lose them.

The doctor has no distinguishing features: his function is merely to be a reliable witness.

This reaction is extreme and melodramatic. The Victorian reader of the book may have found this response more believable than you may do, as a stricter moral code than ours would have made the immoral behaviour appear even worse.

Here, Enfield threatens to 'name and shame' the man. In Victorian times, reputation was very valuable. Today, you could think of social media being used in a similar way.

Edinburgh was associated with having a very serious mindset because of a strict type of Scottish Christianity.

Irony: Enfield's comical simile and his use of exaggeration give an ironic tone to the part of the account.

DO IT!

List what you learn of Hyde's appearance from the extracts on this page. What does the language suggest about his personality?

Extract 2

> "He is not easy to describe. There is something wrong with his appearance; something displeasing, something downright detestable…He must be deformed somewhere; he gives a strong feeling of deformity."

Each item in the list about Hyde's oddness is worse than the one before it. Stevenson uses alliteration with a hard 'd' sound to make Enfield's opinion sound more insistent.

There are many references to Hyde's 'deformity'. Here, the point is repeated for emphasis. Victorians often believed deformity showed moral weakness.

DEFINE IT!

apothecary – doctor

credit – good reputation

Sawbones – nickname for a doctor

undertook – promised

 STRETCH IT!

Why does Stevenson provide so little precise description of Hyde?

Character and theme essentials

NAILIT

Having a wide and precise **vocabulary** will help you to write successful answers in your exam. Write down words you would use to describe each character, then use a thesaurus to find synonyms, exploring the subtle differences between them.

Time

This novel was written in 1886 during the reign of Queen Victoria. In the Victorian age, Britain was successful in the world, building an Empire (see page 68), men had more power than women (who were not yet able to vote) and there was a confident belief in facts and figures.

There were strong views on morality and religion was well-respected. 'Respectable' people believed that a good reputation was very important. However, **hypocrisy** existed: historical information shows that prostitution, drug-taking and alcohol use were high among particular groups. Stevenson explores this double standard through this novel.

Stevenson

Stevenson himself had suffered in his attempts to live up to the expectations of others. He studied law in an effort to please his father, but was not committed to it. His parents were Scottish Calvinists (much like the unemotional doctor in this chapter) but he struggled with belief in God and finally told his parents that he could not believe; they were gravely disappointed, because unbelief would have meant, in their eyes, that their son could not go to heaven after death.

Mr Utterson

Utterson is an unlikely hero. Stevenson has created him to represent the views and values of respectable Victorian morality. He is middle-aged, serious and unexceptional. His work as a lawyer tells us that he follows rules and should be trustworthy and reliable. He takes on a detective-style role within the **plot** and it is his concern that causes him to 'investigate' Hyde. However, he is often wrong in his opinions – for example, thinking that Hyde is after Jekyll's money.

Which **adjectives** would you apply to the characters of Utterson, Enfield and Hyde?

Choose one colour for each character and shade the boxes that apply.

You may find that some adjectives are useful to describe more than one character.

Key:

Utterson	• mysterious	• determined	• commanding
Enfield	• knowledgeable	• callous	• concerned
Hyde	• moral	• loyal	• discreet

Place

The novel is set in London, which at that time was the centre of the British Empire. It was a place of great contrasts in power and luxury, poverty and crime. Victorian readers would be familiar with other novels set in London and the different areas of the city would have had clear reputations for being wealthy, poor, dangerous or fashionable. The daytime Sunday walks present a better view of the city but Stevenson uses the night time street scenes to create a sense of darkness and menace associated with Hyde.

REVIEW IT!

1 Which character opens the novel?

2 What does he mean by 'let my brother go to the devil in his own way'?

3 Who is Mr Enfield?

4 Answer True or False for these statements about the walks taken by Utterson and Enfield.
- Enfield and Utterson talk a lot. ☐
- They take place every Sunday. ☐
- Sometimes they walk with other people. ☐
- If there is work to do, the walks are cancelled. ☐

5 The walks are described as the 'chief jewel of each week'. Which literary device is used here and what does the language suggest about their time together?

6 In which city do the characters live?

7 The door to the cellar is described in detail. Tick the two details that you think best evoke a sense of decay about the doorway. Explain your choices.
- 'Tramps slouched in the recess' ☐
- It had 'neither bell nor knocker' ☐
- 'it was blistered and distained' ☐
- 'children kept shop upon the steps' ☐

8 At what time of day was Mr Enfield returning home?

9 It doesn't say in the novel, but why do you think he is out at this time?

10 What does this suggest about his character in comparison to Mr Utterson?

11 Why was the girl running in the street at night?

12 How did she and 'the man' collide?

13 Which word is used to describe his treatment of the child: bumped/crushed/hit/trampled?

14 Mr Enfield 'took to his heels' after the man. What does he mean?

15 Who else deals with 'the man'? How does this person respond to 'the man'?

16 What do they force him to do?

17 Mr Enfield was curious about the building and its occupant so he 'studied the place'. What does he find out?

18 What is the name of the person who hurt the child?

19 What does Enfield remember most about him?

20 Why do you think Stevenson has started the novel with this account?

Chapter 2
Search for Mr Hyde

The mystery of Dr Jekyll's will

Summary

Utterson returns home after his walk and takes Henry Jekyll's will from his safe to re-read (as a lawyer he would keep this for a client). Utterson is troubled because Jekyll has ordered that Hyde must inherit his property and money if Jekyll should disappear or die. (Here, Stevenson gives us the reason for Utterson's curiosity to find out about Mr Hyde.)

Utterson visits Dr Lanyon, a friend of both himself and Jekyll. Lanyon is described as 'hearty' and 'boisterous'. Utterson mentions Jekyll and discovers that Lanyon had fallen out with him over a matter of science, some ten years previously. Lanyon claimed that Jekyll had become 'unscientific'. Utterson mentions Hyde, but Lanyon has not heard of him.

Utterson returns home but 'he tossed to and fro' unable to sleep because of his 'toiling mind'. He eventually begins to dream, creating versions of the event in which Hyde trampled over the young girl. He also dreams of Jekyll lying asleep and being controlled by a figure with 'no face'. (This supernatural dimension is another key feature of the Gothic literature genre. It could be enjoyed in the same way as you might enjoy the features of a particular genre of film, for example, a chase sequence in an action movie – the audience know what to expect and they enjoy it for what it is.)

Utterson decides that he must see Mr Hyde for himself.

Uncertainty

Lanyon introduces the idea that Jekyll may be unusual or that he holds unacceptable scientific views (many Victorians feared and strongly disapproved of science). Stevenson creates mystery by *not* saying precisely what the argument was about. Lanyon says that Jekyll was 'wrong, wrong in mind'. Like Hyde in Chapter 1, Jekyll is introduced through the eyes of other characters. Stevenson places the reader in the role of detective and encourages us to predict or piece together fragments of information.

Dream

The dream sequence adds to the sense of evil about Hyde. This is an interesting tactic of the author: the character, Hyde, has not done these things, but the reader associates them with him because they are mentioned.

DO IT!

1 Find three short **quotations** that show Dr Lanyon's character and explore the connotations they offer.

2 Explore how these words and phrases from the dream sequence help to convey a sense of menace.
   a 'the gross darkness of the night'
   b 'the curtains of the bed plucked apart'
   c 'glide more stealthily through sleeping houses'

Extract 1

Mr Utterson is concerned about the will and his mind keeps returning to it.

> Utterson has genuine concern for Jekyll and it is dominating his thoughts. Stevenson frequently repeats references to Utterson's anxiety. He describes his spirits as 'sombre' and how he sits down to eat 'without relish', which suggests he is unable to stop thinking about Jekyll and carry on with his normal routine.

> That evening Mr Utterson came home to his bachelor house in sombre spirits, and sat down to dinner without relish. It was his custom of a Sunday, when this meal was over, to sit close by the fire, a volume of some
> 5 dry divinity on his reading desk, until the clock of the neighbouring church rang out the hour of twelve, when he would go soberly and gratefully to bed. On this night, however, as soon as the cloth was taken away, he took up a candle and went into his business room.
> 10 There he opened his safe, took from the most private part of it a document endorsed on the envelope as Dr Jekyll's Will and sat down with a clouded brow to study its contents.

> Notice how the simplicity of the vocabulary used for verbs reflects how plain and simple Utterson's routine is.

> This is intended to impress upon the reader that Utterson cannot let the topic go – he feels he has a responsibility for Jekyll's welfare, both as a friend and as a lawyer.

> It may seem strange to us to make yourself read something that is 'dry' which suggests boring as well as serious. Stevenson is setting Utterson up as a character who does things because they are thought to be right rather than because he naturally wants to do them. This is in keeping with the values of Victorian morality.

> Stevenson creates a complex sentence which includes long adverbials and noun phrases to slow the pace of Utterson's actions, reflecting how reluctantly he approaches this topic.

DO IT!

1 Write three things that you learn about Utterson's lifestyle from extract 1. Explain what Stevenson wants to convey about him from these details.

2 Utterson is behaving differently from usual at this point in the novel. What does this suggest is happening to him? Try to offer two ideas.

STRETCH IT!

Utterson has a representative role in the novel as well as behaving as a character within the plot. This scene could be representative of a Victorian gentleman's lifestyle. Why might it be viewed as commendable by Victorian society? And, why may it be unappealing to both a Victorian and a modern reader?

DEFINE IT!

bachelor – single man

cloth was taken away – when dinner was cleared away

relish – enjoyment

soberly – 'not under the influence of alcohol' also means 'serious'

sombre spirits – serious mood

volume of some dry divinity – a serious religious book

First meetings are key moments in the novel. Pay close attention to this scene as it may be useful in the exam.

Meet Mr Hyde

Summary

Stevenson describes the London setting. Utterson obsessively waits in the street by the door that Hyde had entered in the previous chapter. We are then given our first direct meeting with Hyde.

The first description is of a man 'small, and very plainly dressed'. (Hyde is often described as being unremarkable, suggesting that anyone could be Hyde. This adds to the air of mystery, but could also hint that there is a Hyde in all of us.) Utterson reaches out to tap him on the shoulder and Hyde 'shrank back with a hissing intake of the breath' and 'did not look the lawyer in the face'. (Even though it is Utterson who is behaving oddly by stalking Hyde, it is Hyde who is made to seem unpleasant and unreasonable.)

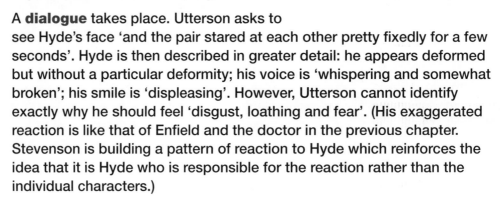

DEFINEIT!

deformed – shaped differently to what might be considered 'normal'

supposition – a thought or idea that gives an explanation

A **dialogue** takes place. Utterson asks to see Hyde's face 'and the pair stared at each other pretty fixedly for a few seconds'. Hyde is then described in greater detail: he appears deformed but without a particular deformity; his voice is 'whispering and somewhat broken'; his smile is 'displeasing'. However, Utterson cannot identify exactly why he should feel 'disgust, loathing and fear'. (His exaggerated reaction is like that of Enfield and the doctor in the previous chapter. Stevenson is building a pattern of reaction to Hyde which reinforces the idea that it is Hyde who is responsible for the reaction rather than the individual characters.)

Utterson then tries to call on Jekyll, but is told by his servant, Poole, that he cannot be disturbed. The lawyer returns home 'with a very heavy heart', believing that Hyde is blackmailing Jekyll with some dark secret from his past. He also fears that if Hyde knows about the will, he may cause Jekyll's death so that he can inherit from him. (These are all just suppositions (ideas) and so the chapter ends, like the first one, leaving the mystery open to the reader's **interpretation**.)

DOIT!

Find the description of the London streets in the paragraph beginning, 'And at last his patience was rewarded…'

London is described as having:
a 'low growl' – a sense of underlying, but not dramatic, menace is conveyed here
'solitary' bystreets
'domestic sounds out of the houses'
'streets as clean as a ballroom floor'

Does Stevenson create a balanced image of the city in this paragraph? Why? Explore the language above to explain what Stevenson wishes the reader to feel from these descriptions. One example has been done for you.

Extract 1

After hearing about Hyde through others, the reader is first presented with him directly in conversation with Utterson. At this stage of the novel, Utterson thinks that Hyde is after Jekyll's money. The first-time reader is likely to think so too as there has been no suggestion yet that Jekyll and Hyde are the same person.

Utterson shows a determination that grows throughout the novel.

Stevenson creates a dramatic **hiatus**; there is a moment of suspense for the reader, waiting to see if Hyde will reveal himself.

Utterson fears that Hyde has his mind on killing Jekyll.

Utterson lies, and so steps beyond appropriate moral, gentlemanly behaviour. However, his lie is nothing compared to the lies of Jekyll. Lies and deceit become more frequent as the novel progresses.

"Will you let me see your face?" asked the lawyer. Mr Hyde appeared to hesitate, and then, as if upon some sudden reflection, fronted about with an air of defiance; and the pair stared at each other pretty fixedly
5 for a few seconds. "Now I shall know you again," said Mr Utterson. "It may be useful."
"Yes," returned Mr Hyde, "it is as well we have met; and *à propos*, you should have my address." And he gave the number of a street in Soho.
10 "Good God!" thought Mr Utterson, "can he, too, have been thinking of the will?" …
"We have common friends," said Mr Utterson.
"Common friends," echoed Mr Hyde, a little hoarsely. "Who are they?"
15 "Jekyll, for instance," said the lawyer.
"He never told you," cried Mr Hyde, with a flush of anger. "I did not think you would have lied."
"Come," said Mr Utterson, "that is not fitting language." The other snarled aloud into a savage laugh; and the
20 next moment, with extraordinary quickness, he had unlocked the door and disappeared into the house.

Utterson is stepping outside the boundaries of polite behaviour in his curiosity to see Hyde. This confrontation is presented like two fight contenders preparing to combat – most unlike the genteel behaviour of gentlemen.

Hyde handles the situation very coolly at this point. His use of formal language, *à propos*, implies courtesy and good manners. He can create a facade (mask) of being civilised at will at this point in his **characterisation**.

Utterson is hypocritical here, because he has lied.

Hyde is described in aggressive, animalistic terms, and as having supernatural speed.

DEFINE IT!

à propos – a formal way of saying 'by the way' (from the French phrase)

common friends – know the same people

fronted about – turned to face him

hiatus – a pause

AQA exam-style question

Starting with this extract, explore how Stevenson presents the character, Mr Utterson, to the reader. Write about:

- how Stevenson presents Mr Utterson in this extract
- how Stevenson presents Mr Utterson in the novel as a whole.

[30 marks]

Use the guidance on pages 84–85 to help you plan your answer.

DO IT!

Stevenson often uses language to imply that Hyde is animalistic. What does 'snarled' suggest about Hyde?

Character and theme essentials

Mr Hyde

Firstly, we learn about Hyde through Enfield's account of 'trampling' over the child; then, through the doctor's reaction to him. We learn of Utterson's fears about the will, that Hyde would harm Jekyll in order to inherit his money. So, as readers, we have been led to believe that Hyde is a detestable character even though we have not met him in person in the novel yet. (Hyde is presented from the **perspectives** of other characters. This allows Stevenson to retain a question in the reader's mind as to whether he actually is as the other characters describe him.)

In this chapter, we are told of Utterson's dream in which Hyde appears as an evil supernatural being. Then, we can witness Hyde for ourselves in their 'real' dialogue. Finally, Utterson gives his thoughts about Hyde, repeating his beliefs about how menacing and immoral he is.

DO IT!

Write a paragraph that summarises how Hyde is presented in the first two chapters.

Part of the plot	What do we learn about Hyde?
Utterson's dream	• Utterson's imagination is 'enslaved'. The implication is that Hyde has overpowered his mind even though it is Utterson who controls his own mind. • The figure in the dream can 'glide more stealthily through sleeping houses', giving it supernatural power. • Hyde is described as a human Juggernaut (a huge idol of the Hindu god, Krishna, which was transported through Indian streets on a heavy cart, in front of which worshippers would throw themselves and be crushed). This metaphor associates Hyde with superhuman powers of destruction. In the Victorian mind, India would be unfamiliar and exotic, adding to a sense of fearfulness in the reader.
Dialogue between Utterson and Hyde	• Utterson is stalking Hyde and eventually meets him. The first description of Hyde is simple: he is 'small and very plainly dressed'. But, Utterson immediately feels that Hyde is something against his 'inclination' (liking). Utterson again prejudices the reader against Hyde. • The language used to describe Hyde's behaviours uses animal references: 'hissing intake of breath', 'snarled', 'savage laugh'. • Hyde gives an 'impression of deformity without any nameable malformation'. References to deformity are part of the Victorian **context**, which is very different to our own times. In that time, 'difference' was associated with moral evil.
Utterson's thoughts	• Positioned at the end of the chapter, Utterson's thoughts confirm and emphasise Hyde's sense of evil power. • Utterson thinks that Hyde must have 'black secrets…secrets compared to which poor Jekyll's worst would be like sunshine'. (This simile is typical of Utterson's character as he often places the characters of Jekyll and Hyde as opposites.)

REVIEW IT!

1 What does Utterson usually do on a Sunday evening?

2 What does this routine suggest about his character?

3 Give two reasons why Utterson is unhappy with Jekyll's will.

4 Who lets Utterson into Dr Lanyon's house? What does this show about his social status?

5 Write two things you know about Lanyon.

6 Why has Lanyon fallen out with Jekyll?

7 What do you think Lanyon means when he says Jekyll is 'wrong in mind'?

8 What happens after Utterson falls asleep?

9 Does Hyde really behave as he does in the dream?

10 Why has the author included the dream sequence?

11 Why does Utterson seek out Hyde?

12 How does Utterson find him?

13 What form of writing is used to recount their meeting?

14 What feeling is Utterson left with after meeting Hyde?

15 What is the name of Dr Jekyll's servant?

16 Which part of Jekyll's house does Hyde use?

17 Why does Utterson think Hyde has a hold over Jekyll?

18 What does Utterson mean when he says that Hyde may have 'secrets compared to which poor Jekyll's worst would be like sunshine'?

19 What does Utterson think Hyde will do?

20 'I must put my shoulder to the wheel – if Jekyll will but let me'. What does Utterson intend to do? What does it imply about Utterson?

Chapter 3
Dr Jekyll was Quite at Ease

Dr Jekyll hosts a dinner party

Summary

Utterson attends a dinner party at Jekyll's house. Utterson stays behind after the other guests leave to have a conversation with Jekyll alone.

Jekyll is introduced as almost a complete contrast to Hyde: 'a large, well-made, smooth-faced man of fifty'. However, a short **phrase** is included, 'with something of a slyish cast perhaps'. (This tiny clue may pass almost unnoticed now but becomes important as we learn more about Jekyll at the end of the novel.) The author continues the description to tell us that he had 'every mark of capacity and kindness' and that he had 'sincere and warm affection' for Utterson. Thus, Jekyll is introduced as a positive character. They briefly discuss Lanyon and the disagreement.

Utterson introduces the topic of the will and of Mr Hyde, telling Jekyll that he has discovered something 'abominable' about him. Jekyll does not wish to hear about this and says that nothing will change his mind about the will. He tries to reassure Utterson by saying that he (Jekyll) can be rid of Hyde whenever he chooses. However, he insists that Utterson must act correctly by Hyde: 'I only ask for justice…when I am no longer here.' Utterson reluctantly promises to do this. (It is ironic and hypocritical that Jekyll asks for 'justice' for Hyde. It is not 'just' that he has loosed Hyde's violence upon the world. Stevenson is critical of Victorian double standards.)

Dr Jekyll

We do not meet the character, Dr Jekyll, until Chapter 3 although we have read positive opinions about him from Utterson. This delay has encouraged us to anticipate what he might be like; it is a technique used by Stevenson to create mystery and to provoke the reader's curiosity.

It is a notably short chapter, and the dialogue is shorter than that with Hyde in the previous chapter. However, across the novel we hear more from Jekyll directly, especially in Chapter 10 'Henry Jekyll's Full Statement of the Case', when we understand him better.

Time frame

This chapter begins with 'A fortnight later…' which aims to give a realistic time frame to events. (Stevenson tries to keep a balance between reality and the fantastical in this novel. It is up to you to decide if this is achieved.) Most of the chapters begin with a reference to time, such as 'That evening' or 'Time ran on'.

DO IT!

Stevenson's general presentation of Dr Jekyll is positive, though there are a few clues that there may be something suspicious behind the jolly exterior.

Re-read the chapter from, 'I have been wanting to speak to you…' Look at what Jekyll says and does. Find the clues that suggest he is hiding something, or is at least reluctant to talk to his friend.

Extract 1

The reason Utterson is involved in the story is because of the will. As a solicitor, he would usually have helped a client draw up a will, but he had refused to write Jekyll's because he disapproved of the proposed contents. All Jekyll's possessions would pass to Hyde if Jekyll were absent for more than three months.

In this extract, Utterson presses Jekyll to discuss the will, even though he doesn't want to.

> "I have been wanting to speak to you, Jekyll…You know that will of yours?"
> A close observer might have gathered that the topic was distasteful; but the doctor carried it off gaily. "My poor
> 5 Utterson," said he, "…I never saw a man so distressed as you were by my will; unless it were that hide-bound pedant, Lanyon, at what he called my scientific heresies. O, I know he's a good fellow – you needn't frown – an excellent fellow, and I always mean to see more of him; but a hide-bound
> 10 pedant for all that; an ignorant, blatant pedant. I was never more disappointed in any man than Lanyon."
> "You know I never approved of it," pursued Utterson, ruthlessly disregarding the fresh topic.

Stevenson hints that Jekyll hides his reaction to talking about the will. This will add to the reader's suspicions.

Does Jekyll try to redirect the conversation by introducing a comment about Lanyon? This is the second time that their argument has been mentioned so it must be significant.

Jekyll is presented as weak-willed. He fails to put his intentions into practice: here, he says Lanyon is 'excellent' but he doesn't act on this to re-establish a relationship. Later, he says that he intends to stop taking the potion… but, predictably, fails.

Notice the repetition of insults used about Lanyon. The word 'pedant' impresses upon the reader that Lanyon's views are the more traditional and Jekyll's must be newer, like those of Darwin or Freud (see page 70).

Stevenson's repetition of the syllable 'ant' suggests that Jekyll is hammering home a point.

A Victorian reader would be much more aware of what the 'scientific heresies' might imply.

Utterson does not politely drop the topic of the will – he presses for an answer. 'Ruthlessly' is quite an emphatic adverb to use in terms of a conversation. As in the earlier dialogue with Hyde, he will drop gentlemanly politeness if he needs to. His determination and boldness are developed throughout the novel.

DEFINE IT!

heresies – ideas that contradict religious beliefs

hide-bound – unchangeable, stubborn

pedant – a person who is concerned chiefly with insignificant detail; in this context, it implies that Lanyon is hanging on to ideas that Jekyll considers old fashioned and outdated

DO IT!

It is clear that Utterson genuinely cares for Jekyll, as well as being his lawyer.

1 List at least four other occasions on which Utterson shows this care for Jekyll.

2 Is Utterson a good friend to Jekyll? Write a paragraph using **evidence** from the novel to support your opinions.

Character and theme essentials

Dr Henry Jekyll

We learn most about Jekyll from the final chapter of the novel when we read his full statement of the case.

At this point, we have been given the opinions of Lanyon and Utterson, and now we have met Dr Jekyll in person.

1 For each quotation in the table, write who says it and what it shows you about Jekyll.

Who says this?	Quotation	What does the quotation suggest about Jekyll?
Utterson	'I thought it madness…now I begin to fear it is disgrace.'	Utterson fears that Jekyll may have done something he regrets in his past.
	'…it is more than ten years since Henry Jekyll became too fanciful for me. He began to go wrong, wrong in mind…'	
	'This Mr Hyde…must have secrets of his own…secrets compared to which poor Jekyll's worst would be like sunshine.'	
	'Dr Jekyll…a large, well-made, smooth-faced man of fifty, with something of a slyish cast perhaps…'	
	'The large handsome face of Dr Jekyll grew pale to the very lips and there came a blackness about his eyes.'	

2 Are the following statements about Jekyll's will true or false?

a Jekyll wrote his own will. ☐

b The will comes into effect if Jekyll is missing for three months. ☐

c Jekyll must die for Hyde to have his property. ☐

d Hyde will have all of Jekyll's property. ☐

e Utterson refuses to help carry out the instructions in the will. ☐

f Utterson promises to carry out the instructions in the will. ☐

REVIEW IT!

1 How many people attend Jekyll's dinner?

2 Why does Utterson linger after the others leave?

3 'Hosts loved to detain the dry lawyer, when the light-hearted and loose-tongued had already their foot on the threshold.' What does this mean?

4 Why do you think Stevenson included this description?

5 Find the quotation that tells you that Jekyll was pleased to have Utterson stay longer than the others.

6 What does Jekyll look like?

7 How does Jekyll respond when Utterson first mentions the will?

8 Jekyll then answers Utterson 'a trifle sharply'. What does this imply?

9 What happens when Utterson first mentions Hyde to Jekyll?

10 'Make a clean breast of this in confidence; and I make no doubt I can get you out of it.' What does Utterson want Jekyll to do?

11 How does he think he can help Jekyll?

12 What does Jekyll plead for Utterson to do?

13 Jekyll says 'the moment I choose, I can be rid of Mr Hyde'. Explain how this comment proves to be ironic by the end of the novel.

14 What have you learned about Utterson and Jekyll's friendship from this chapter?

15 Write a short paragraph to explore whether Jekyll's behaviour in this chapter shows that he is 'wrong in mind' as Lanyon says he is.

Chapters 4 and 5

Chapter 4: The Carew Murder Case

Summary

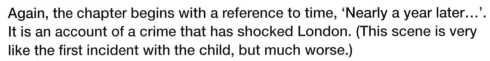

Again, the chapter begins with a reference to time, 'Nearly a year later…'. It is an account of a crime that has shocked London. (This scene is very like the first incident with the child, but much worse.)

The maid describes seeing, in the early hours of the morning, from her upper floor window 'an aged and beautiful gentleman' walking along the street from one direction. He encounters another man, a 'very small gentleman', approaching from the opposite direction. They spoke and she recognised Mr Hyde (who had once visited the house – and whom she had not liked). Hyde burst out 'in a great flame of anger' and furiously beat the older man with his heavy cane. The maid could hear the bones shatter and she fainted.

The victim had been carrying a letter to Utterson so this is brought to him, unopened, by a police officer. He confirms the victim as Sir Danvers Carew – a well-known and important person – by seeing the body at the police station. (Another coincidence with a letter. These feature throughout the novel and have a variety of **structural** functions (see page 80).)

Hearing of Hyde's involvement, Utterson takes the police officer to Hyde's house. The door is opened by an old woman with 'an evil face' who shows them Hyde's room and reports that he was often away from home. The room had been 'ransacked' in a hasty escape and a cheque book burned in the grate of the fire.

The chapter ends with a reminder from the author. People who had seen Hyde could not consistently describe his appearance but they all agreed on one point: 'the haunting sense of unexpressed deformity with which the fugitive impressed his beholders'. (Stevenson would have been familiar with the novels Frankenstein (1823) and The Portrait of Dorian Gray (1890) which both explore the topic of whether external appearances are reflections of morality or immorality – a controversial topic in the Victorian era.)

This act of murder has similarities to the trampling of the child in Chapter 1.

1 What similarities can you find between what happens in these events?

2 How has Stevenson used the choice of verbs ('broke out', 'clubbed', 'trampling', 'hailing down') and adverbials ('with ape-like fury', 'stamping with his foot', 'brandishing the cane') to magnify the violence in this second description?

 STRETCH IT!

What is Stevenson's purpose in choosing to create two such similar examples of Hyde's violent nature?

Extract 1

The description of the murder is narrated by the author, but is seen through the eyes of the maid. This perspective gives Stevenson the opportunity to make the event more sentimental and dramatic for the reader, rather than a 'facts-based' news report.

The setting is literal, the moon is shining, but also metaphorical, it is as if heaven is identifying Carew with a halo-like light.

The choice of verbs establishes a dreamy, calm atmosphere at first.

It is a convenience of the plot that Hyde has visited the house before.

The murder weapon is placed in the foreground and, along with the movement of 'trifling', increases tension and **foreshadows** an ominous event.

The maid's description of Sir Danvers Carew refers to him as 'beautiful' and full of 'politeness' – he is placed in an iconic role as a perfect Victorian gentleman, in opposition to Hyde.

The change is sudden and unprovoked. This conjures up images of an animal or primitive response.

> ...the moon shone on his face as he spoke, and the girl was pleased to watch it, it seemed to breathe such an innocent and old-world kindness of disposition, yet with something high too, as of a well-founded self-content. Presently her eye
> 5 wandered to the other, and she was surprised to recognize in him a certain Mr Hyde, who had once visited her master and for whom she had conceived a dislike. He had in his hand a heavy cane, with which he was trifling; but he answered never a word, and seemed to listen with an ill-contained
> 10 impatience. And then all of a sudden he broke out in a great flame of anger, stamping with his foot, brandishing the cane, and carrying on (as the maid described it) like a madman. The old gentleman took a step back, with the air of one very much surprised and a trifle hurt; and at that Mr Hyde broke
> 15 out of all bounds, and clubbed him to the earth. And the next moment, with ape-like fury, he was trampling his victim under foot, and hailing down a storm of blows under which the bones were audibly shattered and the body jumped upon the roadway. At the horror of these sights, the maid fainted.

Carefully chosen verbs and adverbials convey the violence of Hyde's attack.

Allegedly, the maid could hear the bones shatter. As a critical reader, you may doubt that the maid actually heard these sounds. Stevenson uses her point of view to increase the horror of Hyde's deeds.

STRETCH IT!

Why has Stevenson chosen this person to be Hyde's victim?

AQA exam-style question

Hyde is presented as a character of menace and violence.

Starting with this extract, explore how the author presents Hyde as a menacing and violent character. Write about:

- how Stevenson presents Hyde in this extract
- how Stevenson presents Hyde in the novel as a whole.

[30 marks]

DEFINE IT!

audibly – can be heard

conceived a dislike – grown to dislike

disposition – personality/way of being

trifling – fiddling

Chapter 5: The Incident of the Letter

Summary

On the same day as he has identified the body of Sir Danvers Carew, Utterson visits Jekyll 'late in the afternoon'.

Jekyll is in his laboratory, conveniently located at the end of his garden with a door to the street. The room is carefully described as strange and unpleasant, 'lying gaunt and silent', with 'tables laden with chemical apparatus'. Jekyll looks 'deathly sick' and speaks with 'a changed voice'. (This laboratory environment and the knowledge that Jekyll is an experimental scientist would conjure horrors for some Victorian readers. Some scientists dissected corpses, experimented upon themselves, or argued that the Christian version of creation was untrue: all of these things were shocking at the time.)

Utterson asks Jekyll if he is hiding Hyde. Jekyll replies that he is not and is certain that Hyde has completely disappeared and would never be heard of again.

Jekyll passes Utterson a letter said to be written by Hyde. He asks Utterson to take charge of it and to decide whether or not to show it to the police. The letter contains an apology to Jekyll for having behaved badly when Jekyll had put so much effort and trust in him ('a thousand generosities'). However, there is no envelope; Jekyll had burned it and he says that the letter had been delivered by hand. Utterson believes that Jekyll himself had had a 'fine escape' from being murdered by Hyde. But, as he leaves, he asks Jekyll's servant, Poole, if anyone had delivered a letter by hand that day. No one had. His suspicions are aroused and 'his fears renewed'.

That evening, Utterson asks his clerk, Mr Guest, to take a look at the handwriting of Hyde's letter. Coincidentally, a handwritten invitation from Jekyll arrives at the same time. Mr Guest notes the similarity of the handwriting styles, pointing out particular details which would suggest they had the same author. Utterson recommends that Guest does not mention this to anyone and thinks 'Henry Jekyll forge for a murderer!' and 'his blood ran cold in his veins'. Utterson places the duties of friendship above duty to the law. His loyalty to his friends, emphasised in Chapter 1, is being tested.

Mystery and tension

The author is increasing the sense of mystery and the potential discovery of a terrible secret in this scene. As a modern reader, you may already have been aware of the story, knowing that Jekyll and Hyde are the same person, but we need to be aware of how the readers at the time of publication would have received this information; Stevenson leaves clues for the reader that can be brought together at the end.

DO IT!

What clues have been laid in this chapter to raise the suspicions of a Victorian reader?

Extract 1

Utterson visits Jekyll to decide upon a path of action because he is the lawyer for both the dead man and for Jekyll.

> Jekyll's language focuses on 'promising'. The value of a promise is based on the reputation of the person that promises to be trusted. His repetition has the sound of desperation to it.

" ''Utterson, I swear to God,'' cried the doctor, ''I swear to God I will never set eyes on him again. I bind my honour to you that I am done with him in this world. It is all at an end… mark my words, he will never more be heard of.''

5   The lawyer listened gloomily; he did not like his friend's feverish manner. ''You seem pretty sure of him,'' said he; ''and for your sake, I hope you may be right. If it came to a trial, your name might appear.''

''I am quite sure of him,'' replied Jekyll; ''I have grounds for
10   certainty that I cannot share with anyone. But there is one thing on which you may advise me. I have – I have received a letter; and I am at a loss whether I should show it to the police. I should like to leave it in your hands, Utterson; you would judge wisely…''

15   ''I cannot say that I care what becomes of Hyde; I am quite done with him. I was thinking of my own character, which this hateful business has rather exposed.''

Utterson ruminated a while; he was surprised at his friend's selfishness, and yet relieved by it. ''Well,'' he said at last, ''let
20   me see the letter.'' "

> Stevenson continues to present Utterson as unexcitable and trustworthy, even in this extreme situation.

> Utterson warns that Jekyll's reputation might be damaged if a court case mentions Jekyll as a good friend of Hyde's. At this point, Utterson seems to overlook the fact that a man has been murdered, and reputation seems to be more important than catching a criminal.

> Jekyll pretends to be honest by showing Utterson the letter. However, he is completely dishonest (having forged the letter) and is transferring the problem to Utterson.

> Jekyll is concerned about his reputation.

> Utterson is 'relieved' that Jekyll is focused on keeping his good name.

> Utterson becomes complicit by looking at the letter. Clearly, he has chosen to help Jekyll rather than to have Carew's murderer pursued.

> He uses a **euphemism** to refer to murder – making it seem less horrific.

AQA exam-style question

Starting with the extract above, explore how Stevenson presents the theme of respectability in the novel.

Write about:

- how Stevenson presents respectability in this extract
- how Stevenson presents respectability in the novel as a whole.

[30 marks]

Use the guidance on pages 84–85 to help you plan your answer.

Character and theme essentials

The laboratory and cabinet

Dr Jekyll's laboratory is the location of many scenes in the novel. It had once belonged to a surgeon who used to practise dissecting bodies there. At the time, dissection was seen by the general public as a grotesque thing to do.

Stevenson describes the laboratory and the cabinet room above.

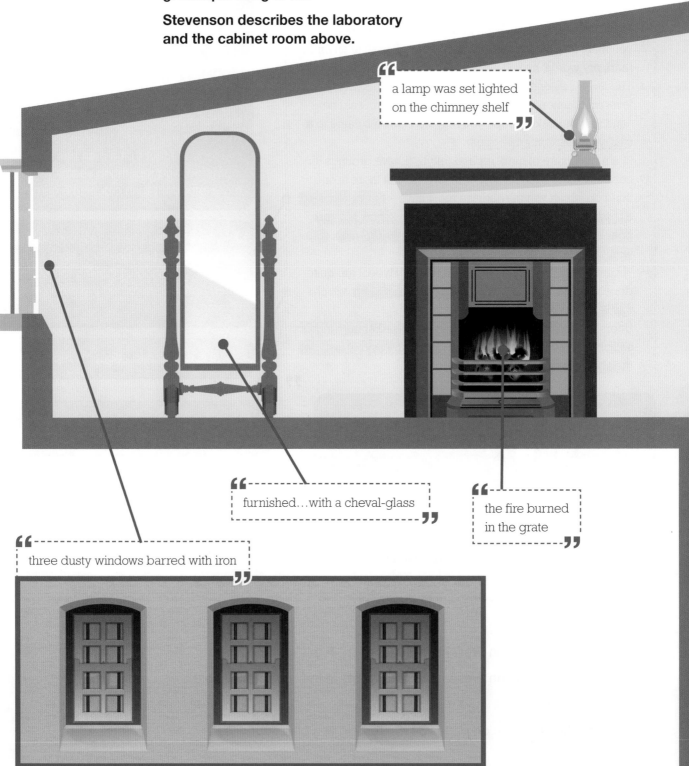

"a lamp was set lighted on the chimney shelf"

"furnished…with a cheval-glass"

"the fire burned in the grate"

"three dusty windows barred with iron"

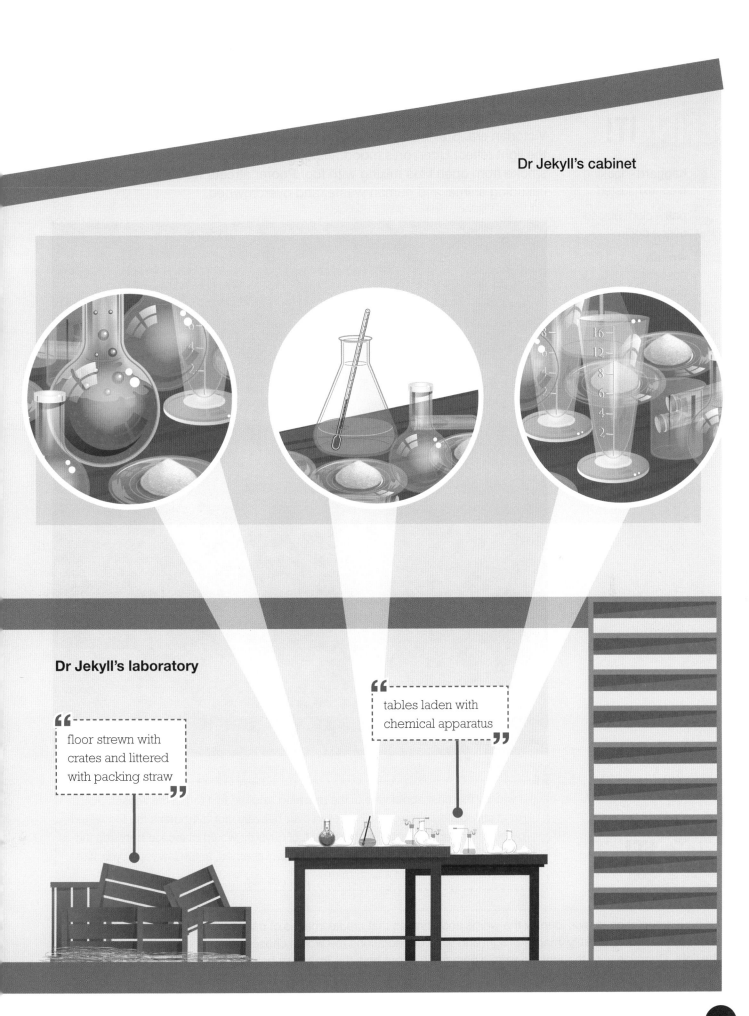

Dr Jekyll's cabinet

Dr Jekyll's laboratory

"floor strewn with crates and littered with packing straw"

"tables laden with chemical apparatus"

London

Stevenson often uses the London setting to create an atmosphere of menace or decay. It is as if the location adds to the mood of the characters or to the general sense of evil. After the murder, Utterson travels to Hyde's house in Soho with a police officer. Soho was known for vice and crime in the Victorian era. Stevenson uses pathetic fallacy by having the description of the light reflect Utterson's mood. Victorian London was smog-filled with the smoke from open fires mixing with fog. Poorer streets would have been dirty, including animal and human waste, and overcrowded.

DEFINE IT!

haggard – looking tired, exhausted

pall – cloth placed over a coffin

wreath – coverings (alternative meaning – wreath of flowers)

DO IT!

> It was by this time about nine in the morning, and the first fog of the season. A great chocolate-coloured pall lowered over heaven…for a moment, the fog would be quite broken up, and a haggard shaft of daylight would glance in between the swirling wreaths. The dismal quarter of Soho…seemed, in the lawyer's eyes, like
> 5 a district of some city in a nightmare.

Using the quotation above, identify the words and phrases that create images of darkness. What kind of darkness is described? Next, identify images of light and what connotations the words chosen suggest about the quality of the light. Combine your thoughts to write a paragraph about how the **imagery** helps to reflect Utterson's sense of dread on the journey to Hyde's home.

REVIEW IT!

Chapter 4: The Carew Murder Case

1
> London was startled by a crime of singular ferocity and rendered all the more notable by the high position of the victim.

Explain in your own words the two reasons why this crime shocked the people of London.

2 Who witnessed the murder?

3
> never had she felt more at peace with all men or thought more kindly of the world

Why has Stevenson included so much unusual detail in the account of the murder?

4 What does the old gentleman look like?

5 What did the old gentleman do when he saw Hyde?

6 What did Hyde do in response?

7 What could the maid hear?

8 How did she know it was Hyde?

9 The maid faints and does not wake for three hours. Why is this detail needed in the plot?

10 Why do the police contact Utterson?

11 The journey to Hyde's house is described in detail:
> Mr Utterson beheld a marvelous number of degrees and hues of twilight; for here it would be dark like the back-end of evening; and there would be a glow of rich, lurid brown, like the light of some strange conflagration.

What is the name of the literary device that links descriptions of locations with emotional moods?

12 How does this strange skyscape reflect Utterson's mood?

13 Hyde's house is located in Soho (see page 34). What reputation did this area have in Victorian times?

14 Highlight the details of Hyde's room which are used to show his external respectability to the reader.
> …Mr Hyde had only used a couple of rooms; but these were furnished with luxury and good taste. A closet was filled with wine; the plate was of silver…a good picture hung upon the walls, a gift (as Utterson supposed) from Henry Jekyll, who was much of a connoisseur…

Chapter 5: Incident of the Letter

15 Jekyll is in the laboratory. What had these rooms been used for previously?

16 What was the Victorian public's attitude to this branch of science?

17 Describe Jekyll's appearance when Utterson sees him.

18 What does Utterson fear Jekyll has done?

19 What does Jekyll want Utterson to do?

20 Why does Utterson tell Jekyll that he has had a 'fine escape'?

21 What is the 'ticklish decision' that Utterson has to make?

22 What does he ask Mr Guest to do?

23 What is the outcome?

24 Why does 'the blood run cold' in Utterson's veins?

Chapters 6 and 7

In some editions of the novel, this chapter is called 'Incident of Dr Lanyon'.

Chapter 6: Remarkable Incident of Dr Lanyon

Summary

A reward has been offered for Hyde and many stories of his cruelty have been 'unearthed', but he has disappeared. Meanwhile, 'a new life began' for Jekyll, who has become more sociable and is on friendly terms with Utterson and Lanyon again, just like the 'old days'. (Notably, Jekyll is presented as having an intensified Christian commitment. You will also find that his language often uses religious metaphors.) However, Utterson is suddenly 'denied admittance' to the house on a sequence of days, which arouses his suspicions. After a while, he goes to Lanyon's house to find him unwell, 'his death-warrant written legibly upon his face'. They talk and Lanyon says that he has 'had a shock' and 'shall never recover'. When Jekyll's name is mentioned, Lanyon's hand trembles and his voice becomes 'unsteady' and says that he regards Jekyll 'as dead' to him.

Utterson's suspicions are further aroused. Lanyon refuses to tell what he knows about Jekyll but tells Utterson that he can judge what has happened after he, Lanyon, is dead. Utterson writes to Jekyll to ask why he is not admitted to the house and about this break in relations with Lanyon. He receives a 'mysterious' reply that gives no explanation of the situation with Lanyon, but asks Utterson to 'respect my silence' and not contact him.

A fortnight later, Lanyon dies. He leaves a letter for Utterson but when Utterson opens it, he finds another envelope inside with instructions that it may not be opened unless Jekyll disappears. (The mysteries increase leaving more puzzles and uncertainties for the reader's entertainment.)

Utterson attempts to visit Jekyll but can only talk with Jekyll's servant, Poole, who tells him that Jekyll spends most of his time in his laboratory. After a number of visits, Utterson stops calling on him.

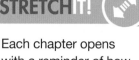

DEFINE IT!

death-warrant – the written instruction that a condemned prisoner would be killed

STRETCH IT!

Each chapter opens with a reminder of how much time has passed. Explain why Stevenson gives such particular references to the passing of time.

DO IT!

Create a timeline of events in Chapter 6 by putting them in the correct order.

- Lanyon tells of a new break with Jekyll.
- Utterson visits Lanyon.
- A reward is offered for Hyde.
- Jekyll dines with friends and supports charity.
- Utterson writes to Jekyll.
- Lanyon dies.

- Utterson visits Jekyll's house less and less often.
- Lanyon is very ill.
- Lanyon, Utterson and Jekyll are all friends again.
- Utterson is repeatedly refused entry at Jekyll's house.
- Jekyll refuses to see him.
- Utterson receives a mysterious package from Lanyon.

Extract 1

Once Hyde has 'disappeared', Jekyll rebuilds his respectable lifestyle. He is transformed.

> Jekyll's interest in religion is increased as the 'evil influence' of Hyde has gone. What might be the reasons for this?

> Now that that evil influence had been withdrawn, a new life began for Dr Jekyll. He came out of his seclusion, renewed relations with his friends, became once more their familiar guest
> 5 and entertainer; and whilst he had always been known for charities, he was now no less distinguished for religion. He was busy, he was much in the open air, he did good; his face seemed to open and brighten, as if with an
> 10 inward consciousness of service; and for more than two months, the doctor was at peace.

> Stevenson lists Jekyll's new pastimes, linking them in one long sentence; this **structure** reflects the way Jekyll's life is 'filling up'.

> It is implied that Jekyll's appearance and health are improved because he is being 'good'.

Jekyll experiences a kind of transformation – back to his old life.

Stevenson suggests that Jekyll's happiness is due to his doing good deeds. This idea would have been central to Victorian Christian thinking.

 **DO IT!**

1 Find two ways that Jekyll would be seen as a 'gentleman' in the eyes of the Victorian readers.

2 In the novel, outward appearances reflect the state of an individual's mind. Happiness or trauma affect how the characters look. In this chapter, Lanyon, too, is transformed, but the reader does not know why. Comment upon Stevenson's choice of adjectives for Lanyon's physical appearance and for his manner in the extracts below. Why is he presenting Lanyon in this way?

Lanyon's appearance when he is first introduced in Chapter 2	Lanyon's appearance after his shock in Chapter 6
This was a hearty, healthy, dapper, red-faced gentleman, with a shock of hair prematurely white and a boisterous and decided manner. At sight of Mr Utterson, he sprang up from his 5 chair and welcomed him with both hands. The geniality, as was the way of the man, somewhat theatrical to the eye; but it reposed on genuine feeling.	The rosy man had grown pale; his flesh had fallen away; he was visibly balder and older; and yet it was not so much these tokens of a swift physical decay that arrested the lawyer's 5 notice, as a look in the eye and quality of manner that seemed to testify to some deep-seated terror of the mind.

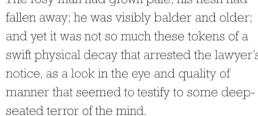 **DEFINE IT!**

arrested the lawyer's notice – grabbed his attention

entertainer – in this context, the host

seclusion – isolation

testify – show

tokens – sign

Chapter 7: Incident at the Window

Summary

Time moves on and Mr Utterson and Mr Enfield take a Sunday walk, passing by the same door as they did at the start of the plot. They enter the courtyard, discussing Hyde, and find Dr Jekyll at the window above them, looking like a 'disconsolate prisoner'.

DEFINE IT!

abject terror – absolute terror

disconsolate – sad

STRETCH IT!

Explain why Stevenson has used the 'Sunday walk' scenario twice in the novel.

A short conversation about Jekyll's health takes place, with Utterson telling Jekyll he should get outside more often. Jekyll talks with them and even manages a smile, but then suddenly 'the smile was struck out of his face' and followed by 'an expression of such abject terror and despair' which 'froze the blood of the two gentlemen'. The window is quickly shut and Jekyll disappears. (Stevenson continues to use emotional reactions typical of those within the Gothic literature genre. A modern reader may find these exaggerated.)

Incidents

Three of the chapters include 'incident' in their title. This cannot be a coincidence so we should consider what they have in common. Remember that the full title of the novel is *The Strange Case of Dr Jekyll and Mr Hyde*.

These three chapters all include events that retrospectively point to the identity of Jekyll and Hyde being one and the same.

1 Look back at the other chapters and remind yourself of the 'incident' that can be seen to prove the case that Dr Jekyll and Mr Hyde are the same person. One example has been done for you.

Chapter	Proof
5 'Incident of the Letter'	
6 'Remarkable Incident of Dr Lanyon'	
7 'Incident at the Window'	The transformation is taking place and the fearful expression is shown on Jekyll's face.

2 This scene shares its location and a number of other similarities with the opening scene. Make a list of similarities and differences between the two scenes.

Extract 1

Stevenson sets a tone for the 'Incident at the Window' through description of location.

> Stevenson sets the scene using pathetic fallacy (see page 76) to suggest the emotion of the character, Jekyll.

> " The court was very cool and a little damp, and full of premature twilight, although the sky, high up overhead, was still bright with sunset.
> The middle one of the three windows was halfway open; and sitting close beside it, taking the air with infinite sadness of mien, like some
> 5 disconsolate prisoner, Utterson saw Dr Jekyll. "

> Jekyll is presented with sympathy. His separation from the life he once had is shown by his position at the window – he is a prisoner whereas the other men are free to live in the wider world.

DEFINE IT!

infinite – never ending

mien – expression

taking the air – getting some fresh air

Extract 2

Although Jekyll has rejected him, Utterson still sees him as a friend.

Jekyll is polite and smiling – it makes him seem calm and sane after his ranting about sinners and suffering in his last letter to Utterson.

Stevenson uses repetition for emphasis.

Signs of reality are juxtaposed with the unnatural events.

"Why then," said the lawyer good-naturedly, "the best thing we can do is to stay down here and speak with you from where we are."

"That is just what I was about to venture to propose,"
5 returned the doctor, with a smile. But the words were hardly uttered, before the smile was struck out of his face and succeeded by an expression of such abject terror and despair, as froze the very blood of the two gentlemen below. They saw it but for a glimpse for the window was
10 instantly thrust down; but that glimpse had been sufficient, and they turned and left the court without a word. In silence, too, they traversed the bystreet; and it was not until they had come into a neighbouring thoroughfare, where even upon a Sunday there were still some stirrings of life, that Mr
15 Utterson at last turned and looked at his companion. They were both pale; and there was an answering horror in their eyes. "God forgive us! God forgive us!" said Mr Utterson. But Mr Enfield only nodded his head very seriously, and walked on once more in silence.

The metaphor of 'struck' makes it seem as if violence has been done to Jekyll.

The expression is described in **abstract nouns** rather than in specific physical detail. This is more typical of Gothic literature than modern, more **naturalistic, styles**.

We learn more about the reaction of the onlookers than what happened to Jekyll. Stevenson uses commonly used metaphors.

Utterson strangely says, 'God forgive us!' as he has nothing to be forgiven for. It could be a reference to the Lord's Prayer.

Enfield and Utterson are shocked into silence and are both pale with fear or concern.

AQA exam-style question

Does Stevenson encourage the reader to feel sympathy for Jekyll?

Starting with the extract above, explore your opinions about Stevenson's presentation of Jekyll. Write about:

- how Stevenson presents Jekyll in this extract

- how Stevenson presents Jekyll in the novel as a whole.

[30 marks]

Use the guidance on pages 84–85 to help you plan your answer.

Character and theme essentials

Friendship

The three key characters in the novel are bachelors – unmarried men. We learn that they socialise by dining with one another and enjoy conversation. This may be with others: 'the doctor gave one of his pleasant dinners to some five or six old cronies, all intelligent, reputable men, and all judges of good wine', but these other men do not feature as characters. There is no suggestion that any women attend their gatherings.

The liking and respect between the three of them is stated several times by Stevenson.

1 Which values are shown in the friendships between the men?

loyalty   competition   curiosity   confidentiality   patience   protectiveness

2 Which other combination of characters in the novel have a good friendship?

3 Tick to show who is being referred to in the quotation.

	Mr Utterson	Dr Lanyon	Dr Jekyll
a Whose friends 'were of his own blood or those whom he had known the longest'?			
b Who 'became once more their familiar guest and entertainer'?			
c Who were being described when the author writes 'in the old days when the trio were inseparable friends'?			
d Who said, 'We three are very old friends, Lanyon; we shall not live to make others'?			

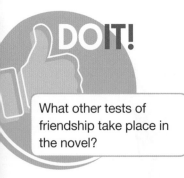

Test of friendship: Lanyon and Jekyll

The first argument between two of this group of 'oldest friends', Lanyon and Jekyll, causes a separation that lasts ten years. It is over a point of science. Even Utterson cannot understand it. Strangely, however, he does not react as if it is a major upset, which clearly it must have been. The second separation occurs in Chapter 6 'Remarkable Incident of Dr Lanyon', and follows a period of renewed friendship between the two scientists. This time, Lanyon declares that Jekyll is 'dead' to him and seems to associate Jekyll with fear as his 'face changed' and he 'held up a trembling hand'.

What other tests of friendship take place in the novel?

STRETCH IT!

Refer to the section on the Victorian historical context, respectability and repression on page 69.

What do you learn about Victorian values from the friendships between the men?

Chapter 6: Remarkable Incident of Dr Lanyon

1 Hyde's past was 'unearthed'. What does this mean?

2 Stevenson does not state Hyde's misdeeds. He allows his reader to imagine them. What do you think his Victorian readers may have imagined when Stevenson referred to them? Complete the table below.

Quotation	What a Victorian reader may have imagined
'cruelty'	
'vile life'	
'strange associates'	

3 How did the murder of Carew first affect Utterson? How is he now time has passed?

4 Utterson thinks that the death of Carew was 'more than paid for by the disappearance of Hyde'. What does this mean?

5 How do you feel about Utterson justifying the death in this way?

6 Give two examples of how Jekyll has changed since Hyde disappeared.

7 'The trio were inseparable friends'. Who were the trio?

8 When Utterson visits Lanyon, what physical changes does he notice?

9 Utterson thinks Lanyon has a 'terror of the mind'? What do you think he means by this?

10 Lanyon predicts his own death and says it is because of a shock. How might a Victorian reader and a modern reader react to this?

11 How does Lanyon refer to Jekyll?

12 Utterson receives a letter from Jekyll. Summarise what it says.

13 After the funeral, Utterson opens a package from Lanyon. What is in it? What is the message on the front? What does this remind Utterson of?

14 True or false?
- Utterson's attitude to Jekyll changes. ☐
- Utterson looks forward to talking to Jekyll. ☐
- Poole gives news of Jekyll. ☐
- Utterson never gives up visiting him. ☐

Chapter 7: Incident at the Window

15 How does the following description of the evening imply Jekyll's emotional state?

> The court was very cool and a little damp and full of premature twilight, although the sky, high up overhead, was still bright with sunset.

16 What is the name of the literary device that associates the environment with the emotions of a character?

17 What does Utterson ask Jekyll to do?

18 Why does Jekyll smile?

19 How does his face change?

20 Enfield and Utterson were pale and 'there was an answering horror in their eyes'. Stevenson uses this technique of giving the reactions of others to emphasise moments of horror at Hyde's presence. Write down some other examples of this.

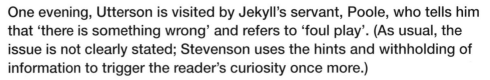

Where is Dr Jekyll?

Summary

One evening, Utterson is visited by Jekyll's servant, Poole, who tells him that 'there is something wrong' and refers to 'foul play'. (As usual, the issue is not clearly stated; Stevenson uses the hints and withholding of information to trigger the reader's curiosity once more.)

Utterson goes to Jekyll's house with Poole, where he finds all the servants huddled together and distressed. Poole takes Utterson into the laboratory building and up to the 'cabinet'. Poole tells the person inside that Utterson is there to see him and a voice answers. Both know that this is not Jekyll's voice. Utterson is described as being 'very pale' and nervously 'biting his finger' but he cannot find any logic in a murderer staying in the laboratory if Jekyll has been killed. Poole then recounts the events in the household across the last week.

Poole has been sent out across the city with letters to various chemists requesting particular drugs to be supplied. The letters are in Dr Jekyll's handwriting. Poole also describes seeing Jekyll 'cry out like a rat' and run away from him. (Remember that in the context of Victorian England, 'shopping' would have to be done by sending out letters – it was not a strange thing for Jekyll to do.)

Utterson tries to find a rational explanation suggesting that Jekyll is suffering from an illness that deforms him. However, Poole insists that Jekyll has been murdered and so Utterson thinks it is his duty to find out by breaking down the door.

Utterson is clearly not an 'action hero'. This chapter is his most 'active' role.

Make a list of all the things that Utterson does during the novel. Are any of them heroic in your opinion?

Utterson's character

One of Utterson's roles in the story is to provide a realistic, clear-thinking commentary on the fantastical events of the plot – we are meant to trust his logical mind. At these points it may seem strange to us that the 'hero' of the tale is a middle-aged lawyer who is known for his seriousness.

Extract 1

Poole and Utterson are outside the cabinet, having just spoken to the person within to ask if Utterson can see Jekyll. But the voice that answers does not sound like Henry Jekyll.

"

"Sir," he said, looking Mr Utterson in the eyes, "Was that my master's voice?"

"It seems much changed," replied the lawyer, very pale, but giving look for look.

5 "Changed? Well, yes, I think so," said the butler. "Have I been twenty years in this man's house, to be deceived about his voice? No, sir; master's made away with; he was made away with eight days ago, when we heard him cry out upon the name of God; and *who's* in there instead of him, and *why* it stays there, is a thing that cries to Heaven,

10 Mr Utterson."

"That is a very strange tale, Poole; this is a rather wild tale my man," said Mr Utterson, biting his finger. "Suppose it were as you suppose, supposing Dr Jekyll to have been – well, murdered, what could induce the murderer to stay? That won't hold water; it doesn't commend itself

15 to reason."

"

Poole questions Utterson whereas it is usually Utterson who questions others or himself.

Utterson's reaction has been seen on other occasions. Can you recall them?

Poole voices his concern. This may also be the Victorian reader's deduction at this point. The modern reader is probably less surprised.

The references to crying to God and Heaven for deliverance from evil emphasise the theme of religion and good and evil at this most intense point in the plot. Here, Hyde is associated with possession by a devil - an idea that Victorians would have been familiar with from stories in the Bible.

Utterson is sensible and critical – as he was at the beginning of the novel. But he is clearly nervous as shown by this uncharacteristic repetition of words or ideas.

Using the extract above, identify examples of Utterson:

- showing emotion
- asking critical questions
- making statements of opinion.

AQA exam-style question

Mr Utterson is the only possible hero in this novel.

Starting with this extract, explore whether the author presents Utterson as a hero of the novel.

Write about:

- how Stevenson presents Utterson in this extract
- how Stevenson presents Utterson in the novel as a whole.

[30 marks]

Use the guidance on pages 84–85 to help you plan your answer.

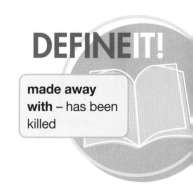

made away with – has been killed

Chapter 1

The death of Dr Jekyll

Summary

Armed with a poker and an axe, Utterson and Poole head for the cabinet door, recognising that they are about to place themselves 'in a position of some peril'. Poole admits that his intuition recognised evil and he could give his 'bible-word' that the figure was, indeed, Hyde. Poole describes the figure as having been 'like a monkey', fast-moving and leaving him with a feeling that 'went down my spine like ice'.

Two other servants, Bradshaw and 'the boy', are placed on guard at the back entrance to the laboratory in case the figure should try to escape. The moon is hidden and the sky is dark. Steps can be heard pacing up and down the room. Utterson demands that Jekyll come out but it is Hyde's voice that answers, so Poole breaks the door with an axe while a 'screech, as of mere animal terror' is heard from within.

Inside the room there is a mixture of normality (a fire, tea laid out) and laboratory ('presses full of chemicals'). The body 'of a man sorely contorted and still twitching' lies dying on the floor, holding a 'crushed phial' as evidence of suicide ('a self-destroyer').

The body wears Jekyll's clothes, which are far too big for it. Poole and Utterson search the building for Jekyll's body without success. They then turn their attention to the chemicals, notes written by Jekyll into a book and to the key to the outside door that has been stamped upon and broken. (Clearly, Stevenson is collecting clues for the reader's attention, just like a scene from a detective story.)

Finally, an envelope addressed to Utterson is opened and Utterson goes home to read the contents, saying that he will be back before midnight, when he would 'send for the police'. (This will seem strange to us today as it would not be natural to leave the servants in the house with the corpse; we would expect to call the police to take over investigations immediately.)

Give a reason for each object being in the room.

mirror

fireside and chair

key

Extract 1

Utterson and Poole have entered the cabinet to find Hyde dead upon the floor.

"

The besiegers, appalled by their own riot and the stillness that had succeeded, stood back a little and peered in. There lay the cabinet before their eyes in the quiet lamplight, a good fire glowing and chattering on the hearth, the kettle
5 singing its thin strain, a drawer or two open, papers neatly set forth on the business table and nearer the fire, the things laid out for tea; the quietest room, you would have said, and, but for the glazed presses full of chemicals, the most commonplace that night in London.
10 Right in the middle there lay the body of a man sorely contorted and still twitching. They drew near on tiptoe, turned it on its back, and beheld the face of Edward Hyde. He was dressed in clothes far too large for him, clothes of the doctor's bigness; the cords of his face still moved with
15 a semblance of life, but life was quite gone; and by the crushed phial in the hand and the strong smell of kernels that hung upon the air, Utterson knew that he was looking on the body of a self-destroyer.

"

The entry to the room has been violent.

But, inside the room Stevenson has created a scene of conventional normality – cosy, warm, well-ordered. Why has he done this?

In contrast, the body is presented as grotesque. Hyde is said to be dead, but he is still moving.

Poole and Utterson have to move the body to confirm its identity. Notice the use of the pronoun 'it' not 'him'.

Once again, the difference in size is noted. Now that Hyde is dead, he is less fearsome. Does this seem grotesque or pathetic?

In keeping with the plot, Hyde uses poisonous chemicals for his suicide. Is there any irony in the fact that chemicals gave life to him and now take it away?

tea tray with cup and plate

packet of letters

religious book

DEFINEIT!

besiegers – attackers

contorted – twisted

kernels – in this context, they could refer to cyanide, the poison taken by Hyde

phial – small glass container

riot – violence

self-destroyer – suicide victim

semblance – appearance

DOIT!

Highlight the details that describe Hyde's physical reactions. Do you feel sympathy for him, or do you consider this to be a suitable punishment?

Character and theme essentials

Action and hiatus

This chapter is notable for its great sense of drama. It is visually easier to imagine because each action is made **explicit**. In other parts of the novel, actions are withheld from the reader and left to our imaginations: we see only two of Hyde's crimes as most are just referred to as wickedness; we often see the emotional response of a character but little of their physical behaviour. So, this action-packed chapter is perhaps easier and more engaging for a modern reader.

Imagine, then, the effect on the Victorian reader who would not have had films or television on which to view this kind of suspense and drama. Stevenson uses his slow reveal technique by pausing the action – creating a hiatus – at various points to achieve the best manipulation of his readers – for their own enjoyment.

DO IT!

1 Find the moments of hiatus that Stevenson uses in this chapter to make the action happen in identifiable 'steps'. Make a copy of the table below to list them. One has been done for you.

Moment of increased drama	How Stevenson delays the climax of the action
Poole mentions 'foul play'.	After this moment, Utterson and Poole then trek across London. Stevenson uses pathetic fallacy to create a description of deserted, windswept streets with the wind so strong that it 'made talking difficult'. Thus, the notion of 'foul play' is allowed to run through the reader's imagination, generating greater anticipation.
Poole accuses the 'thing' in the laboratory of murder.	
Poole describes a thing that cried out like a rat and ran away.	
Utterson decides that they will enter the laboratory.	
Finally, they enter the laboratory.	

2 The last chapter, 'Henry Jekyll's Full Statement of the Case' is made up of reflection (thoughts about the past) and physical actions. Which chapters would you consider to have more or less physical action? Using a different colour for each, shade each chapter as having low, medium or high intensity of action. You may think some chapters have a mixture. This task will help you to have an overview of the novel as a whole.

Can you explain how Stevenson controls his narrative and his reader by using this **structure**?

1 Story of the Door
2 Search for Mr Hyde
3 Dr Jekyll was Quite at Ease
4 The Carew Murder Case
5 Incident of the Letter
6 Remarkable Incident of Dr Lanyon
7 Incident at the Window
8 The Last Night
9 Dr Lanyon's Narrative
10 Henry Jekyll's Full Statement of the Case

REVIEW IT!

1 Why has Poole come to see Utterson?

2 Poole sits with 'wine…untasted'. Why does Stevenson include Poole's reluctance to speak?

3 Utterson has 'a crushing anticipation of calamity'. What does this mean?

4 The journey had been through deserted streets but when they arrive at Jekyll's house Stevenson describes:

> The square…was all full of wind and dust, and the thin trees in the garden were lashing themselves along the railing.

Why does Stevenson delay the description of the weather until they arrive at Jekyll's?

5 Before they open the door to the house, Utterson says, 'God grant there be nothing wrong', and Poole replies, 'Amen.' How does this exchange link to the theme of religion in the novel?

6 What happens when Poole and Utterson open the door to the hallway of the house?

7 Why does Stevenson include this background scene?

8 Put these events in the correct order.

- Poole declares that there is 'a thing' in the laboratory. ☐
- Poole signals Utterson to make no noise. ☐
- Poole asks if Utterson may see Jekyll. ☐
- Poole takes Utterson to the laboratory building. ☐
- Utterson thinks Jekyll's voice is much changed. ☐

9 Utterson questions the logic of Poole's 'wild tale'. What does this show about Utterson's character? What is the effect on the reader?

10 Poole has a note. What is it about?

11 Utterson questions why Poole has an opened note as it would have been unacceptable for a servant to have opened a master's note. Why do you think Stevenson has included this detail?

12 Utterson comes to one of his wrong conclusions as to why Jekyll seeks out the drug. What is his explanation?

13 Poole has seen the person in the laboratory and believes that he is not Jekyll. What makes him think this?

14 Poole describes the person as a 'masked thing like a monkey'. How is this typical of other descriptions of Hyde? Recall another example of this type of language.

15 Utterson's language: 'Well, let our name be vengeance' echoes a verse from the Bible, '"Vengeance is mine," says the Lord' (Romans 12:19). Why has Stevenson used biblical language here?

16 Poole says that he heard the person 'Weeping…like a lost soul'. How does this add to the religious theme?

17 What other clues does Poole use to convince Utterson that it is not Jekyll in the room?

18 What do they see when they break down the door? Why has Stevenson created the scene in this way?

19 Why are these things in the room?

Traces of chemical work	
A religious book with shocking comments written on it	
A large mirror	
An envelope addressed to Utterson	

20 > If your master has fled or is dead, we may at least save his credit.

What does Utterson mean? When has he behaved like this before? Which theme does it link to?

Dr Jekyll's letter

Summary

This chapter contains a document written by Dr Lanyon, which also includes a letter written to him from Jekyll. The letter asks Lanyon to carry out a series of mysterious instructions, including breaking into Jekyll's cabinet to get some 'powders, a phial and a paper book'. These objects should then be taken to Lanyon's home where a man would be sent to collect them.

Lanyon narrates how he entered Jekyll's cabinet and describes the chemicals and notebooks he finds there. He realises that he is dealing with 'a case of cerebral disease' (insanity) but wonders why Jekyll could not have sent his messenger to collect the items from his house himself.

Lanyon then waits at his home for the mysterious messenger. He arms himself with a revolver. At midnight the messenger, Hyde, arrives. (Midnight is in keeping with Gothic conventions.) He is described as 'small' but with 'great muscular activity' and a 'shocking expression' on his face.

Chemicals and experiments

Many of the Victorian general public thought of scientists with fear and suspicion. True stories of people being murdered to provide bodies for scientific dissection and of scientists carrying out experiments upon themselves horrified society. Some experiments were performed for public entertainment and education by scientists who either needed the finances or the exposure to get their ideas recognised.

In Jekyll's laboratory, Lanyon finds:

- powders of Jekyll's private manufacture
- a simple crystalline salt of a white colour
- a phial about half full of a blood-red liquor
- phosphorus
- volatile ether
- 'At the other ingredients, I could make no guess'.

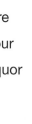

Mental illness

The identification of mental illness increased considerably across the 19th century though not in terms that we would consider to be accurate today (for example, phrenology used the bumps on someone's head to assess their character and character deficiencies). Treatment generally meant locking people up in institutions. Thus, Lanyon is probably prepared to try to help Jekyll to avoid this fate if possible.

DO IT!

How might you expect a Victorian reader to react to the listing of Jekyll's chemicals?

Extract 1

Jekyll's letter to Lanyon aims to persuade him to go to the laboratory and collect his chemicals. To be persuasive, Jekyll emphasises the bonds of friendship between them.

> "You are one of my oldest friends; and although we may have differed at times on scientific questions, I cannot remember, at least on my side, any break in our affection. There was never a day when, if you had said to me,
> 5 "Jekyll, my life, my honour, my reason, depend upon you," I would not have sacrificed my fortune or my left hand to help you. Lanyon, my life, my honour, my reason, are all at your mercy; if you fail me tonight, I am lost."

It seems strange that Jekyll and Lanyon have not spoken for ten years, but Jekyll still considers them to be friends.

The 'scientific questions' probably challenge the accepted view of the world at that time, such as Darwin's theory of evolution (see page 70).

The last time we heard Jekyll comment on Lanyon, it was to insult him as a 'pedant'. This seems to be hypocrisy in an attempt to persuade Lanyon to help.

Jekyll refers to noble, abstract concepts to try to persuade Lanyon. He also repeats himself, as he often does with words and phrases. He adds reasons one after the other in lists to pressure Lanyon to agree.

The tone here is typical of Jekyll – it is dramatic and he uses **hyperbole** (exaggeration). He places the responsibility for events onto Lanyon in his attempt to get Lanyon to help him.

DEFINE IT!

affection – friendship

Extract 2

At the end of the letter, Jekyll adds a further note.

> "I had already sealed this up when a fresh terror struck upon my soul. It is possible that the post-office may fail me, and this letter not come into your hands until tomorrow morning. In that case, dear Lanyon, do
> 5 my errand when it shall be most convenient for you in the course of the day; and once more expect my messenger at midnight."

The tone is even more dramatic – using religious imagery – emphasising Jekyll's desperation.

Letters have played a significant role in controlling the plot. Here, the mention of the post office and late deliveries gives the moment more reality.

Jekyll is being particularly polite and formal in an attempt to persuade.

Typical mystery and suspense are created as Lanyon must wait and expect an unknown visitor…at midnight!

DO IT!

Write a brief paragraph to explore the **rhetorical devices** that Jekyll uses to persuade Lanyon to help him.

The transformation

Summary

The visitor, Hyde (although Lanyon does not know this at first), asks for the items from Jekyll's house and proceeds to mix the chemicals. Stevenson describes this in some detail so that the reader can easily visualise the scene. The person then challenges Lanyon to witness new knowledge that would 'stagger the unbelief of Satan'. (The challenge is spoken in language that would fit in a fairy tale: 'Will you be wise? Will you be guided?...or has the greed of curiosity too much command of you?' It is also the language that Satan uses in the Garden of Eden to tempt Eve.) Lanyon accepts the challenge, saying that he has taken part in these unusual events so far and that he wants to see what the end will bring. Hyde reminds him that his vows as a doctor would mean that he could tell no one of what he sees.

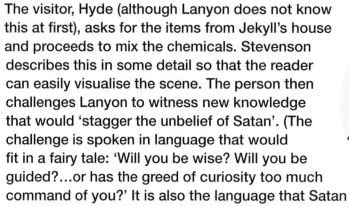

Hyde drinks and a violent transformation from one body form to another takes place: 'he reeled, staggered, clutched at the table...gasping with open mouth' and Lanyon is 'submerged in terror'. (This is one of a series of climaxes in the plot. It contains the horror element of the Gothic genre.)

At the end, Jekyll stands in the room and tells Lanyon that the other 'form' that was there was, in fact, Mr Hyde – the murderer of Carew. Thus, Lanyon knows they are the same person and is horrified.

Extract 1

Hyde taunts Lanyon when he visits him at night. This conversation addresses the relationship between the scientists in the novel.

> "It is well," replied my visitor. "Lanyon, you remember your vows: what follows is under the seal of our profession. And now, you who have so long been bound to the most narrow
> 5 and material views, you who have denied the virtue of transcendental medicine, you who have derided your superiors – behold!"

The vow refers to the promise of confidentiality between a patient and a doctor. It is misapplied here for the sake of the narrative.

Ironically, it is Jekyll who is actually enslaved, or 'bound' by his addiction to the freedom to be Hyde.

'Behold' reminds the reader of the language of the Bible but, ironically, also a magician's trick or a scientist theatrically performing a public experiment.

Hyde speaks with great arrogance and taunts Lanyon with 'you...you... you' and refers to being 'superior'.

Hyde refers to the argument between Jekyll and Lanyon some ten years previously.

In real life, Victorian scientists debated and argued over the new approaches to science. The passion for one form over another was real. Lanyon represents the old view of Christian creation, whereas Jekyll and Hyde represent the shocking, new science that challenged accepted beliefs that most people did not want to have questioned.

Adam and Eve

Victorian readers would have studied their Bibles or learned from these stories at church. In this Christian story, Adam and Eve (the first humans God created) live in an idyllic place called the Garden of Eden where all is good. Everything is provided for them and they have one rule to obey: Do not eat from the tree of knowledge. Eve is tempted by a snake to try the fruit of the tree. She tempts Adam to taste it too. God then expels them from Eden and they suffer because now they know both good and evil, and are no longer 'innocent'.

 **STRETCHIT!**

The Bible story of Adam and Eve and the tree of knowledge would have been well-known to the Victorian reader.

Explain how both Lanyon and Jekyll are tempted by the desire for knowledge in this scene.

Extract 2

Next, the transformation from Hyde to Jekyll takes place.

> He put the glass to his lips and drank at one gulp. A cry followed; he reeled, staggered, clutched at the table and held on, staring with injected eyes, gasping with open mouth; and as I looked, there came, I thought, a change – he seemed to swell – his face became suddenly black and the features seemed to melt and alter – and the next moment I had sprung to my feet and leaped back against the wall, my arm raised to shield me from that prodigy, my mind submerged in terror.

Stevenson crowds this section with verbs to create a sense of energy, urgency and horror.

Adverbials add more physical actions – this is a highly visual scene.

There is a supernatural feel in the transformation. These things would not be possible. But, to the Victorian reader, things we now accept would have been thought impossible too (for example, organ transplantation).

Stevenson uses the metaphor of drowning to convey how overwhelming the experience is.

Lanyon's reaction is used to emphasise the horror of the situation, but his physical reaction is of no use against the mental trauma he will suffer as a witness to this event.

A moment of hiatus relieves the intensity of this scene, allowing the reader to pause and get ready for the climactic moments.

 AQA exam-style question

Starting with this extract, explore how the author creates tension.

Write about:

- how Stevenson creates tension in this extract
- how Stevenson creates tension in the novel as a whole.

[30 marks]

Use the guidance on pages 84–85 to help you plan your answer.

Character and theme essentials

Horror: Gothic literature

Gothic literature is a genre of writing that focuses on fear, horror, death and love. Emotions are likely to be intense and descriptions of nature are often used to suggest the emotional background to events.

The Gothic literature genre had begun in the 18th century and continued to be popular throughout the 19th century. Mary Shelley published *Frankenstein* in 1818 and Oscar Wilde published *The Portrait of Dorian Gray* in 1890. Both of these novels, like *The Strange Case of Dr Jekyll and Mr Hyde*, deal with the relationship between creator and subject.

The stories contained similar patterns of 'ingredients', which we call Gothic conventions. Think about how a television, YouTube or book craze grows and spawns others that are similar. Gothic stories became popular in this way – because they worked for the audiences of the time.

We still enjoy Gothic conventions in media, and some elements have even been turned into 'Goth' fashion.

DO IT!

Can you find any of these Gothic conventions in *The Strange Case of Dr Jekyll and Mr Hyde*?

Write an example for the conventions that you find. One has been done for you.

Convention	Present in the novel? Yes/No	Example from the novel
Dark, mysterious locations		
Madness		
Isolation		
Terror		
Intense emotions		
Doppelganger (doubles)		

Ghosts		
Supernatural elements	Yes	Transformation scenes - especially in front of Lanyon, and Jekyll's description of the first transformation
Secrets		
Imprisonment		

REVIEW IT!

1 Who has written a letter to Dr Lanyon?

2 Why is Lanyon surprised to receive a letter?

3 ❝

> Lanyon, my life, my honour, my reason all are at your mercy; if you fail me tonight, I am lost.

❞

What does Jekyll's language show about his state of mind?

4 Where is Lanyon asked to go?

5 Why must he go there?

6 After he returns, what should he do?

7 Why does he agree to do this?

8 What does Lanyon find in the package?

9 Give two reasons why the visitor looks strange to Dr Lanyon.

10 What makes Lanyon feel an 'icy pang along my blood'?

11 How might the reader respond to this?

12 ❝

> I could hear his teeth grate with the convulsive action of his jaws.

❞

What impression is created of Hyde here?

13 What is Hyde impatient to do?

14 What offer does he make Lanyon?

15 What is Lanyon's answer?

16 What does he see?

17 'there stood Henry Jekyll'. How might a reader respond to this moment?

18 How does Lanyon feel at the end of this experience?

19 ❝

> What he told me in the next hour I cannot bring my mind to set on paper.

❞

Why has Stevenson chosen to withhold Jekyll's explanation here?

20 Lanyon is traumatised by the 'moral turpitude' that Jekyll told him of. What does 'moral turpitude' mean?

Chapter 10
Henry Jekyll's Full Statement of the Case

Dr Jekyll describes his background

Summary

The next narrative is presented as written by Dr Jekyll and we assume that it is the second document that Utterson reads, although we never hear from Utterson or the narrator again.

It is a complex part of the book, tracking Jekyll's history and thoughts.

1 Jekyll gives some basic personal background: he was born wealthy, handsome ('endowed with excellent parts'), hard-working and keen to be respected – an ideal Victorian gentleman.

2 However, he speaks of a 'gaiety of disposition' (a liking for pleasure in his life) which he disapproves of and which he tries to hide, creating a 'profound duplicity of me', meaning his life is like an untruth or lie.

3 He then 'scientifically' discusses how a person, or self, is made of more than one part.

4 He questions whether greater happiness for each self could be achieved if they were separated.

5 His 'theory' is then helped by some insights 'from the laboratory table' as to how the parts could be separated. The 'temptation' of his discoveries causes him to put ideas into practice and so he experiments with chemicals.

6 However, he withholds his methods for two reasons: because of the burden this knowledge places on the person who knows it; because his work was 'incomplete' and so should not be shared.

7 Jekyll's transformation is described. It is painful and vivid. He views himself in a mirror to find that his new, immoral character's form is 'shrunken'; he believes that this is because he is nine-tenths a good person and only one-tenth bad, so this is shown physically. He drinks the potion again to return to being Jekyll. However, he falls into the 'slavery' of his new power and changes at will. He enjoys committing immoral 'crimes' without his usual conscience stopping him.

8 He refers to the strong reactions of revulsion in others when they meet Hyde (as has been described throughout the story). He explains that Hyde is 'pure evil' and people have not experienced this before as the separate 'selfs' within a person have not been divided in this way before.

9 Jekyll gives a retrospective account of the incident with the child and the murder of Sir Danvers Carew.

10 The details are the same as in the previous accounts, but information about feelings of enjoyment is added.

DO IT!

For each section of the narrative, go back to the novel and find one key quotation. This will help you to follow the plot and the **arguments** that Jekyll makes to justify his choices.

Extract 1

Jekyll describes the murder of Sir Danvers Carew. The tone here is elevated, dramatic and self-pitying, in keeping with Jekyll's tone of voice throughout his other letters.

Psychological theories (like those of Freud) were circulating at the time of the novel; these ideas proposed the idea of different parts to a personality. Interestingly, Jekyll refers to 'my devil'. For the Victorian readers, belief in the devil was also very real.

He explains how the desire to do evil has increased, employing the metaphor of 'escape'.

Jekyll refers to the Day of Judgement when all people must account for themselves to God. Many Christians would fear hell and this would be a motive not to sin.

> My devil had long been caged, he came out roaring. I was conscious, even when I took the draught, of a more unbridled, a more furious propensity to ill. It must have been this, I suppose, that stirred in my soul
> 5 that tempest of impatience with which I listened to the civilities of my unhappy victim; I declare at least, before God, no man morally sane could have been guilty of that crime upon so pitiful a provocation; and that I struck in no more reasonable spirit than that in
> 10 which a sick child may break a plaything.

Jekyll combines religious and natural references to create a metaphor to describe his brutal attack. It has a less **emotive** impact on the reader than the account by the maid. Perhaps Stevenson is showing Jekyll's hypocrisy at preserving a 'better' impression of himself when he is actually confessing to a murder.

Notice the euphemistic language Jekyll uses to refer to the murder of Carew. Jekyll distances himself from the act of 'killing', referring to it with vague vocabulary.

He refers to insanity and compares himself to a child to imply that he is not responsible for his actions.

Extract 2

Here, Jekyll describes his pleasure in the murder… and a turning point.

> With a transport of glee, I mauled the unresisting body, tasting delight from every blow; and it was not till weariness had begun to succeed, that I was suddenly, in the top fit of my delirium, struck through the heart by
> 5 a cold thrill of terror. A mist dispersed; I saw my life to be forfeit; and fled from the scene of these excesses…

DO IT!

1 Explore the effect of these examples on the reader:
  • 'My devil had long been caged, he came out roaring.'
  • He feels a 'tempest of impatience'.
  • He strikes in the way 'a sick child may break a plaything'.
2 Identify and explore the words and phrases that describe Jekyll's reaction to the murder in Extract 2.

DEFINE IT!

civilities – politeness

delirium – madness

draught – potion

forfeit – pay the price of the crime

mauled – tear with claws

propensity – inclination to

provocation – reason to be offended

succeed – take over

tempest – storm

transport – surge

unbridled – unchained

unhappy – poor

STRETCH IT!

Stevenson has created for Jekyll the voice of an educated gentleman. How might this affect a Victorian and a modern reader?

Dr Jekyll's growing addiction

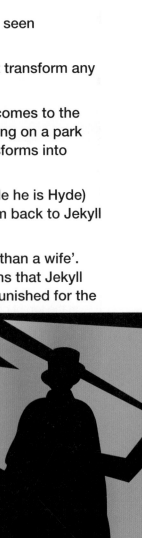

Summary

The list below continues to track Jekyll's account of his experimentation and his thoughts begun on page 56.

11 Jekyll notes a change in the performance of the potion. At first, it was harder to throw off the Jekyll self; it is later reversed and becomes harder to return to being Jekyll.

12 His mind is at war over which self to be: the 'elderly and discontented doctor', Jekyll, or to have the 'liberty, comparative youth, the light step, the leaping impulses and secret pleasures' of Hyde.

13 Like an addict going 'cold turkey', he attempts to quit and live completely without the potion.

14 He fails as his is 'tortured with throes and longings', demanding that he take it again. He gives in 'in an hour of moral weakness'.

15 The murder of Carew means that Hyde can no longer be seen anywhere (because if he is seen, he will be arrested).

16 This gives a 'sense of joy' to Jekyll because he *must* not transform any more.

17 However, despite his efforts to live morally, the evil self comes to the surface when he is not actively suppressing it; while sitting on a park bench, enjoying memories of his wicked deeds, he transforms into Hyde – without the potion.

18 Jekyll then recounts the event of visiting Dr Lanyon (while he is Hyde) to get the last of the chemicals that may work to turn him back to Jekyll (as told in the previous chapter, 'Dr Lanyon's Narrative').

19 Jekyll finds that 'insurgent horror was knit to him closer than a wife'. Hyde's self is growing stronger and dominant. This means that Jekyll has to live inside the cabinet so as not to be seen and punished for the murder.

20 Jekyll's part of the self falls into 'despondency' (depression) and grows weaker.

21 Hyde hates the Jekyll part of the self and so torments it by spoiling things and ideas that were once important to Jekyll (for example, the picture of his father).

22 However, Jekyll holds the power of suicide which could stop Hyde.

23 Jekyll ends this statement by writing that he does not know what may happen next (though as the reader, we know that he is dead by this time).

For each section of the narrative, go back to the novel and find one key quotation. This will help you to follow the plot and the arguments that Jekyll makes to justify his choices.

Extract 1

Jekyll has stopped taking the potion but finds that the transformation can happen without it.

Stevenson uses pathetic fallacy to set a 'positive' scene to increase the contrast with what happens next.

This 'impure' thought opens him up to the physical transformation. Notice how the pace increases through the use of a list.

Stevenson uses the idea of a table, laid out for a meal and waiting for the person to return, as a metaphor for stable life.

> It was a fine, clear, January day, wet under foot where the frost had melted, but cloudless overhead; and the Regent's Park was full of winter chirrupings and sweet with spring odours. I sat in the sun on a bench; the animal
> 5 within me licking the chops of memory; the spiritual side a little drowsed, promising subsequent penitence, but not yet moved to begin. After all, I reflected, I was like my neighbours; and then I smiled, comparing myself with other men, comparing my active good-will with the lazy
> 10 cruelty of their neglect. And at the very moment of that vainglorious thought, a qualm came over me, a horrid nausea and the most deadly shuddering. These passed away, and left me faint; and then as in its turn faintness subsided, I began to be aware of a change in the temper
> 15 of my thoughts, a greater boldness, a contempt of danger, a solution of the bonds of obligation. I looked down; my clothes hung formlessly on my shrunken limbs; the hand that lay on my knee was corded and hairy. I was once more Edward Hyde. A moment before
> 20 I had been safe of all men's respect, wealthy, beloved – the cloth laying for me in the dining-room at home; and now I was the common quarry of mankind, hunted, houseless, a known murderer, thrall to the gallows.

Jekyll was thinking back to the misdeeds he had enjoyed doing as Hyde. This time the animal metaphor is used to convey satisfaction rather than violence. He has promised that he will make amends for his wicked ways...but hasn't yet done so.

Stevenson repeats 'comparing' as a criticism of Jekyll who makes a false comparison between himself and others: he thinks himself superior to others because he is going to be better than they are.

As Stevenson often does in the more active scenes of the novel, he creates a hiatus before moving the reader on to another list, this time of the outcome of the transformation.

Another list is used to sum up the contrast between himself and Hyde.

DEFINE IT!

licking the chops – like a dog remembering enjoying a meal, he is enjoying remembering

penitence – a religious term: doing something good to make up for doing bad things

vainglorious – arrogant

qualm – strange feeling

solution of the bonds of obligation – dissolving of the rules of society

thrall to the gallows – due to be hanged

DO IT!

1 Explain how this transformation differs from the others. Why has it happened now?

2 Identify the positive and negative images that Stevenson creates in this section. Why has Stevenson organised this scene to move between positive and negative images?

Character and theme essentials

Science

Through Jekyll, Stevenson has explored a controversial topic of his time. How could new theories from the world of science fit with accepted Christian religious beliefs?

During the century before the Victorians (1700s), a 'natural' or 'scientific' view of the universe had begun to be understood. However, in Christian Europe, it was still generally believed that God had created the universe.

In the book of Genesis, the Bible describes God creating the universe: light, land, water, animals and humans. This view had been held for many hundreds of years and even leading scientists accepted it.

In 1859, Darwin's book *On the Origin of Species*, argued that the world was the product of evolution – changes over time – and not instantly created by God. This was considered blasphemy (speaking against the word of God) and Darwin suffered a lot of criticism and isolation because of this. However, within decades, his interpretation was being widely accepted.

Victorian England was fearful of science because it was exposing doubts in the Christian explanation of the world – a belief that many accepted and felt 'safe' with. Jekyll represents the 'dangerous' scientist:

Jekyll	Why he could be criticised
His laboratory was once a dissecting room.	This links him to those scientists who dissected corpses. This was unacceptable and frightening to many Victorians.
He argues with and is estranged from an old friend because of his beliefs.	Knowledgeable people disagree with him but, in his arrogance, he does not listen.
He appears respectable but his experiments happen in secrecy.	He is deceitful.
He tries to separate his 'self' into parts. He creates another being.	He breaks the laws of nature and of God as creator of the world.
He becomes addicted.	He is guilty of excess and lack of control.
His experiments become out of his control.	Science cannot be controlled and is dangerous.

DO IT!

Most Victorian readers would have read about the creation of the world in the Bible and often heard about it read out loud in church. Now, imagine that, having believed this account all your life, people whom you don't trust are telling you that it is not a true account. How might you feel towards them?

Select from the adjectives below that you think could be applied to a Victorian Christian reader's view of scientists. Look up any you don't know.

untrustworthy   iconoclastic   meddling   destructive   blasphemous   immoral   misguided

REVIEW IT!

1 What did Jekyll think was a fault in his character as a young man?

2 What does he describe as 'the war among my members'?

3 What time of day does Jekyll first try the potion?

4 How does the transformation make him feel?

5 Why does he prefer being Hyde?

6 Why is Edward Hyde so much smaller than Henry Jekyll?

7 What effect does Hyde have on other people?

8 Hyde does 'monstrous' things. Give examples of his evil deeds.

9 Why could Stevenson not describe them in detail?

10 Why does Jekyll not feel very guilty about what Hyde does?

11 How does the murder of Sir Danvers Carew offer hope for Jekyll?

12 Why does Jekyll lead a life of 'severity' after the murder?

13 What problems begin to occur with the transformations?

14 Describe Hyde's hand.

15 Describe how Jekyll and Hyde spend their final days.

16 " And certainly the hate that now divided them was equal on each side. "

What does this mean?

17 Hyde's terror of the gallows forces him to return to being Jekyll at times. What is the 'terror of the gallows'?

18 Why does Jekyll pity Hyde?

19 What final control does Jekyll have over Hyde?

20 " I bring the life of that unhappy Henry Jekyll to an end. "

Why has Stevenson ended the novel with that clause?

Characters

Dr Jekyll

What do we know about Dr Jekyll?

- Dr Jekyll is a wealthy, educated Victorian scientist.

- He creates a potion that can transform him into an evil version of himself – whom he calls Mr Hyde.

- He tries to rid himself of Hyde but is eventually 'taken over' by this side of his personality.

- He dies when Hyde commits suicide.

Jekyll in middle age

Stevenson wants the reader to like Jekyll as a 'perfect' Victorian gentleman born to a large fortune. However, he hints at there being a darker dimension to his personality.

Jekyll has a circle of good friends who are much like himself. He has a good reputation and a full social life. We learn that he was known for his charity and that he was Christian. Utterson has a high opinion of Jekyll and worries that he is making a will that could place him in danger. (The reader has been guided to trust Utterson and his opinions guide us to respect Jekyll.)

Jekyll's youth

In his full statement (Chapter 10), Jekyll refers to his youth. He found it difficult to live up to his own expectations and those of Victorian society with its many 'rules' on how to lead a good life. (This point links to Freud's concepts of id, ego and superego – see page 70.)

Jekyll likes to appear to be outstandingly moral. He criticises himself for his 'impatient gaiety of disposition' and wants to crush this side of himself.

He refers to being guilty of 'irregularities' of behaviour but also says that other men might have boasted of these actions. (This suggests that the deeds weren't too terrible or that publicly respectable men often privately engaged in immoral behaviour.)

Jekyll's battle

Jekyll's 'morbid sense of shame' leads him to unhappiness with himself. As a scientist, he theorises about and then experiments with separating the 'good' and 'bad' sides of human nature. He describes the 'accursed night' that he made and drank the potion, but also describes his enjoyment of being Hyde and committing pleasurable, wicked deeds without conscience.

DO IT!

Do you agree or disagree with the statements below? Provide evidence for your opinions.

- Jekyll is a model Victorian gentleman.

- Jekyll represents good and Hyde represents evil.

- Stevenson has created the character of Jekyll so that he, Stevenson, can criticise Victorian hypocrisy.

Mr Hyde

What do we know about Mr Hyde?

- Mr Hyde is the alter-ego of Dr Jekyll.

- He is stunted and small, yet powerful and clever.

- He is violent and debauched – eventually committing murder.

- He commits suicide to avoid being captured and hanged for murder.

Physical appearance

There is little detail about Hyde's appearance. He is small – 'pale and dwarfish'. Jekyll says that his life was nine-tenths good and that Hyde is formed from the one-tenth that is bad; for this reason, he is smaller.

Hyde is described as youthful and he can move with 'extraordinary quickness'. Lanyon says that he had a 'great muscular activity and great apparent debility of constitution', appearing both extremely strong but physically small and weak at the same time, suggesting a supernatural quality about Hyde. This is emphasised in Utterson's dream when he imagines Hyde moving swiftly and stealthily through the city, crushing children.

Because there is so little physical description, the reference to Hyde's hand gains importance. Jekyll describes Hyde's hand as 'lean, corder, knuckly,… thickly shaded with a swart growth of hair', whereas his own is 'professional in shape and size…white and comely'. The comparison makes Hyde seem unpleasant, as we now expect. (His hand is 'corded' implying strength, and hairy to suggest primitive or even animal origins.)

Behaviour

We learn of a few of Hyde's crimes – violence to the child, the murder of Carew and hitting a woman in the face – but others are left to the imagination. Stevenson expects his readers to imagine horrors that Hyde has committed.

Hyde is presented through other characters. These begin with Enfield, the doctor and the crowd around the small child who was trampled in Chapter 1. They continue with Utterson, who thinks that Hyde has 'Satan's signature' upon his face, and then Lanyon. Jekyll explains that because Hyde 'was pure evil', people respond to him differently to ordinary humans, who are a mixture of both good and bad.

Animal and devil imagery

Hyde is described using terms such as 'devil', 'Satan', 'spirit of hell'. These terms associate him with the supernatural and so give him a sense of uncontrollable, inhuman power. Stevenson also uses animalistic references: Hyde snarls, hisses, growls and can spring. Jekyll describes him as a devil that had been 'caged' a long time and came out 'roaring'.

DO IT!

Plan a response to the following question: Does Hyde develop as a character during the novel or is he just a representative of evil?

1 First, recall the accounts in which Hyde appears in the novel.

2 Next, note any changes (or not) in Stevenson's presentation of him.

3 Consider whether there are changes in Stevenson's presentation of him, or whether it is only the evil he does that changes.

Comparison of Jekyll and Hyde

	Jekyll	Hyde
What's in a name?	A reference to the word 'kill' can be seen in Jekyll's name. Ironically, he is both a killer (of his first self, Jekyll) but he is the creator of the other self (Hyde) in the novel.	Mr Hyde does hide from the reputable social circle of Utterson and Lanyon. But, he is also the hidden side of Dr Jekyll. (He could represent what Victorian society knew about itself but wanted to keep hidden.)
Separate characters?	They are presented as separate characters. Jekyll refers to them being like a father and son but, according to Jekyll's explanation, Hyde is an aspect of Jekyll's self.	
Victim or villain?	Jekyll despises and tries to control something in himself. The Victorian attitude to this 'repression' of character would be different to our own times (where accepting yourself is more valued). His attempts to do this lead to his experiments and then addiction to the transformations and opportunities these hold. Jekyll suffers in attempts to remove Hyde from his life and we may sympathise with him as he describes his agonies as an addict.	Hyde is presented as evil and isolated. While there is little opportunity to see him as a victim, he is an aspect of Jekyll, enabling him to explore his depraved pleasures but shift the blame. The accounts we hear are all about Hyde, and the most information about him is presented by Jekyll in Chapter 10. It is for readers to judge whether they attribute Hyde's crimes to him as a separate character, or as a part of Jekyll.
What do they represent?	Jekyll represents a view of life held by the Victorian middle class. He appears to be responsible, reputable, well-liked and living in a virtuous way by supporting charity and religion. However, the fact that this is not his whole self represents the hypocrisy of Victorian middle-class society. (See page 68 for more information about the Victorian context.)	Hyde represents a variety of ideas that were considered alien or unacceptable by the Victorian middle class. Hyde can represent the undesirable side of a self that exists within all people. The idea that this self may grow beyond control would have been a source of fear for Victorian readers. The increasing urban working-class poor were thought to be immoral and brutal. Hyde behaves in this way. Exploration of the world brought stories of 'savages' whose customs would not be acceptable to the Victorians. Hyde threatens Victorian superiority with his violence and lack of conscience.

Mr Utterson

What do we know about Mr Utterson?

- Mr Utterson is a lawyer and trusted friend of Dr Jekyll.
- His concern for Dr Jekyll leads him to track down Mr Hyde.
- He learns of Hyde's misdeeds through other characters he knows: Mr Enfield, Dr Lanyon and Sir Danvers Carew.
- Mr Utterson eventually breaks down the door to Hyde's hiding place and discovers his dead body.

Role

Much of the story is seen, heard or read from Utterson's perspective. The story itself is quite incredible (unbelievable) so Utterson is created as a credible witness. Stevenson opens the novel with a portrait of Utterson: 'Mr Utterson the lawyer was a man of rugged countenance that was never lighted by a smile…' It starts by focusing on his seriousness and goodness, and then adds 'lovable' which seems a little surprising. He enjoys a drink – in moderation – but hasn't been to the theatre in twenty years; he is made to seem human but very sensible.

We learn later than he usually reads his Christian articles on Sundays after supper and that he has 'an approved tolerance for others'. This may be why Jekyll confides in Utterson by addressing his full statement to him.

Utterson's role as a lawyer is key to the plot of the novel. He has seen Jekyll's will which worries him and prompts him to make contact with Hyde. Sir Danvers Carew was carrying a letter addressed to Utterson, which triggers Utterson's involvement with the police to visit Hyde's house. Mr Guest, who identifies the similarity between Jekyll's and Hyde's handwriting, is Utterson's clerk, allowing him a smooth entry into the plot.

At the start of the novel, Utterson takes a walk with Enfield and this is presented as the highlight of his week. Later, he stalks Hyde, attends Hyde's home with the police, identifies Carew's body and eventually breaks down the door of Jekyll's cabinet. It is ironic that this sensible lawyer is in some ways the most active character in the novel.

The reader is encouraged to know Mr Utterson, but not to be too interested in him: the focus remains on the mystery of the relationship between Jekyll and Hyde. Initially, the reader learns about them at the same pace as Utterson, though the reader's deductions will eventually outpace Utterson's discovery of the truth.

STRETCH IT!

Why is it important for Utterson to be seen as serious at the beginning? Why is he presented as loyal and persistent in the middle? Why does he need to be presented as assertive and level-headed at the end of the novel?

DO IT!

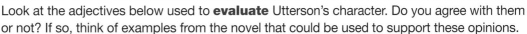

Look at the adjectives below used to **evaluate** Utterson's character. Do you agree with them or not? If so, think of examples from the novel that could be used to support these opinions.

Point in the novel	Are these accurate adjectives for Utterson's characteristics?
Beginning	serious, likeable, trustworthy
Middle	loyal, persistent, inquisitive, protective
End	assertive, determined, level-headed

Dr Lanyon and minor characters

Lanyon

Like Jekyll, Lanyon is a scientist and a doctor. He is introduced as a 'hearty, healthy gentleman…with a boisterous and decided manner'. Although he is an outspoken and bold character, he has 'genuine feeling' (friendship) for Utterson and Jekyll. Stevenson presents Lanyon as a likeable character, and then introduces the idea of an argument between himself and Jekyll. Because he is likeable, and because we meet Lanyon before we meet Jekyll, this throws a little suspicion onto Jekyll's character.

The argument is over science: Lanyon accuses Jekyll of 'scientific balderdash'. The new theories emerging in the Victorian era challenged existing views of religion and caused much controversy and concern. Stevenson's readers would have understood their quarrel. (Lanyon is developed as a personality but he also has a role as a representative of the arguments about science that were taking place in the Victorian era.)

Jekyll is fond of Lanyon, but calls him a 'hide-bound pedant' (someone who is closed to new ideas). When Hyde visits Lanyon to gain the chemicals he needs, he relishes showing Lanyon the transformation. The shock of this hurries Lanyon's death. (Jekyll re-establishes his relationship with Lanyon when he is not taking the potion, suggesting that the scientific argument can be overcome if Jekyll is functioning as a 'civilised' character.)

Enfield

A distant relative to Utterson, Enfield is another respectable gentleman, although being a 'man about town' suggests that he is more worldly than Utterson. He gives an account of the trampling of the child. He features twice in the plot, both times on a Sunday walk with Utterson and by the rear of Jekyll's property. The second time he witnesses Jekyll's expression of horror in the 'Incident at the Window' (Chapter 7).

Poole

Poole is a good servant to Jekyll. He is polite, loyal, discreet and, eventually, brave. While Utterson cannot see Jekyll, Stevenson uses Poole to update him (and the reader) on Jekyll's health and habits. Poole's most significant role is to trigger the events of the 'last night' by his visit to Utterson. Like a narrator, he tells of the quest for chemicals and of the alteration of Jekyll's personality. Finally, he enters the cabinet with Utterson and their dialogue reveals Utterson's amazement and confusion. (Poole's role within the plot is more important than his personality.)

DO IT!

Is *The Strange Case of Dr Jekyll and Mr Hyde* essentially a story about middle-aged men? Explain your opinion. Why do you think the story became so popular with its Victorian audience, and continues to be of interest today?

Female characters

Women were frequently presented idealistically as pillars of goodness and morality within Victorian tales. However, women are notable for their absence in *The Strange Case of Dr Jekyll and Mr Hyde*. The women merely exist in the background of the novel – its main focus is the Victorian world of educated men.

When females do appear in the novel, it is as 'types' rather than as formed characters. The girl who is trampled and the woman who is struck in the face by Hyde are female because this intensifies his 'crime'. The Victorian middle-class attitude to women meant that they were supposed to be protected and admired by men and, in turn, they were expected to serve and support men.

Female character		Function
Maid at Carew's murder	The maid who tells of the murder of Carew is said to be 'romantic' (meaning emotional).	Delivers information
Hyde's housekeeper	She is presented as a 'hag' (typical of fairy tales and associated with evil) which means she can withstand Hyde's presence.	Allows access to Hyde's house
Maid at Jekyll's house during 'the last night'	She 'wept loudly', which is used by Stevenson to increase the tension.	Increases tension

REVIEW IT!

1 Who is often described as being animal-like?

2 Give two other negative ways of describing this character.

3 Explain the two ways he is seen to be dressed.

4 What is Hyde intended to represent to the Victorian audience?

5 Where does he live? Why does Stevenson place his house there?

6 Give two examples of Hyde's brutality.

7 What does he do to Jekyll's religious books?

8 Why has the writer included that detail?

9 What does he look like when dead?

10 How does Stevenson add to the horror of his death?

11 In which part of the house does Jekyll carry out his science work? What had it previously been used for?

12 Why has Stevenson chosen this location?

13 What clue does Stevenson give about Jekyll's nature in his first description?

14 How does Stevenson encourage his reader to think of Jekyll positively?

15 What did Jekyll not like about himself and caused him to experiment with separating his personality?

16 Why does Utterson stop visiting Jekyll?

17 How does Utterson unite the novel?

18 What changes happen to Dr Lanyon after he has seen the transformation?

19 What makes Poole a good servant to Jekyll?

20 What is Enfield's function in the novel?

Themes and contexts

This novel is very much a product of its time. It is essential to know about the society, beliefs, discoveries and challenges of the time in which it was written in order to fully understand it.

The Victorian era

Queen Victoria's reign (20 June 1837 until her death, on 22 January 1901). is known as the Victorian era. It was a long period of peace, wealth and commercial exploration to expand the British Empire.

The middle class – people with wealth from professions – was increasing. Christianity was dominant but city crime was also growing. Homosexuality was illegal; women could not vote – neither could many men as votes were based on ownership of property.

There were rigid expectations of behaviour for men, women and children and restrictions on what could be discussed in 'polite society'. Stevenson cannot give details of Hyde's crimes; the graphic description of today's novels or films would have been unacceptable to a middle-class readership. However, cheap **fiction** for the working classes, penny dreadfuls, contained accounts of crimes in greater detail.

Victorian society is remembered for its high morals (expectations of good behaviour) and its hypocrisy (when people or characters claim to have higher standards of behaviour or beliefs than they actually do).

In Chapter 1, Mr Enfield gives his opinion on talking about other people's business to explain why he did not ask Hyde about his use of the door to Jekyll's property.

> No sir: I had a delicacy…I feel very strongly about putting questions; it partakes too much of the day of judgment…

It is not until the final chapters when Lanyon and Jekyll unburden themselves that any open honesty is shown in the novel. Could the tragedies in the novel have been avoided if communication had been more open?

Respectability and repression

The Victorian era was a time of emotional and sexual repression. It was unacceptable to discuss sexuality or express emotions in public. Self-control was key, particularly for men. Even happiness could be a temptation to stray from moral goodness. Reputation – your position in society and how others regarded you – was highly important.

Jekyll tries to fulfil his own and society's high moral standards. However, he is tempted by pleasures. Stevenson does not describe these; he allows us to imagine. All we know is that Jekyll has secrets in his past of which he is ashamed.

Repressing a desire or urge can cause it to grow. After Jekyll's two-month break from taking the potion, Hyde's desires for unacceptable pleasures are stronger, 'My devil had long been caged, he came out roaring'.

Medicine

Controversial medical developments in Victorian times included dissection of corpses to learn more about human anatomy. Dissecting the bodies of executed criminals was legal, but frowned upon by respectable society. Dissections took place in hospital lecture rooms, or on private premises – entering through the rear doors to avoid public notice. (This is suggested by the cellar door at Jekyll's house.)

In addition, the famous criminal case of Burke and Hare – bodysnatchers who ran a trade in corpses for dissection, including murdering victims to provide the dead bodies for surgeons – was well-known. Stevenson plays on his readers' fears that medicine and experimentation were dangerous and unnatural.

Today, successful ground-breaking operations are celebrated in our media and we have closely controlled medical trials to develop new drugs. In the Victorian era, a scientist would have needed a volunteer to try a new drug – some also experimented on themselves, as Jekyll does. Stevenson uses this to paint a picture of an obsessive, perhaps 'mad' scientist who then pays the price of breaking the laws of nature. (Stevenson's readership may have enjoyed the fear created and the fact that Jekyll is punished for his arrogance in challenging God's laws of nature.)

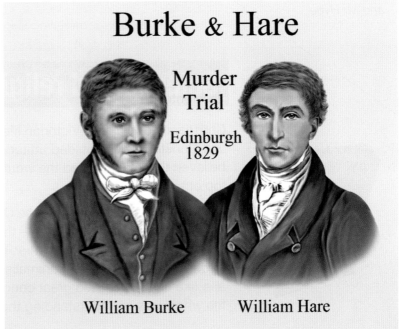

Burke & Hare

Murder Trial

Edinburgh 1829

William Burke   William Hare

Psychology

Stevenson was interested in the workings of the mind, especially in the analysis of dreams and what they might show about the subconscious self. Stevenson explores the idea of a dual nature in this novel: that a person obeys different driving forces.

His idea had some similarity with that of the ground-breaking psychological theories of Sigmund Freud. Though Freud published his theories after this novel, Stevenson would probably have been aware of them.

Freud identified strands of personality that combined to create human behaviours:

- id – seeks pleasure and avoids pain; it is instinctive (and could be thought more primitive)
- ego – responds to social norms and laws of the world around you
- superego – focuses on the desire to fulfil the expectations that you hold for yourself.

(In the novel, Jekyll tries to separate his pleasure-seeking self so that he can focus on fulfilling his own Victorian middle-class expectations of himself.)

DO IT!

Do you agree or disagree with the statements below. Explain your opinion.

1 Stevenson teaches his readers that the instinctive, primitive side of personality should be repressed.

2 Stevenson sends out a warning about the dangers of self-repression in *The Strange Case of Dr Jekyll and Mr Hyde*.

Science and religion

Christianity dominated Victorian life and values. Churches were well attended and Christian values guided attitudes – at least on the surface. Most people believed that God created the world and had placed man (not woman) at the top of the natural order.

Charles Darwin published *On the Origin of Species* in 1859. This book presented the idea of evolution – that species adapted and changed – and that man had evolved from earlier, more ape-like beings. (Remember that Hyde is often described in animalistic terms and that he attacked Carew 'with ape-like fury'.) It caused great concern and fear at the time because, if true, the whole way of understanding the world would be challenged.

Jekyll's experiments represent the side of science that challenged accepted thinking and called into question God's supremacy, and even existence. This would have been scandalous in Victorian times. It could be for this reason that he argues with Lanyon, who may have stuck more closely to the accepted religious view. Stevenson's readers may have been shocked or outraged by Jekyll's attitudes. As modern readers, we probably find that we are not so fearful or critical of scientific discovery.

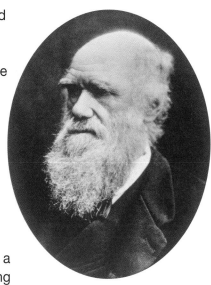

Good and evil

We can try to divide the novel into a battle of good and evil: Hyde representing evil and the other characters representing good. There is no wholly 'good' character but it is easy to find evidence for Hyde's evil. If it is a battle, Hyde does not win as he is forced to self-destruction to escape being hanged for Carew's murder.

So, the battle between good and evil is more likely to be an internal battle than an external one. Hyde and Jekyll are, in fact, two sides of the same self. Stevenson has presented them as separate characters but they are the duality of human nature – we are made of both good and bad qualities.

DO IT!

Here are two responses to the question 'To what extent is Hyde presented as the embodiment of evil?'

Student Answer A

Stevenson selects language that emphasises Hyde as evil. Hyde is referred to as 'devil' or 'Satan'. Victorians were Christian and believed in God and Satan so Stevenson wants them to think Hyde is pure evil by using these names for him.

Student Answer B

Within the Christian framework of Victorian thinking, Stevenson's repeated references to Hyde as 'devil' and 'Satan' would have automatically marked him as evil in the reader's imagination. Even today, with less enforcement of Christian teaching, these references commonly signify evil.

Which answer:

- introduces information about the period in which the novel was written? A ☐ B ☐ Both ☐
- refers to the response of a Victorian reader? A ☐ B ☐ Both ☐
- refers to the response of a modern reader? A ☐ B ☐ Both ☐

Which do you think is the better answer? Explain your opinion.

Location

London was full of contrasts of wealth and poverty. There were well-defined areas of wealth and respectability… or poverty and crime. Stevenson refers to the night-time streets several times: Enfield, Carew and Hyde are all out late or in the early hours of the morning. (Why are the 'respectable' characters out at this time?) Night-time would be associated with real danger and crime. Supposedly respectable men could visit areas of the city to easily find prostitutes and drugs, while pretending to live moral lives at home.

Jekyll's house has one door in a respectable part of town, and the other to a more secret courtyard. His double life is echoed in the construction of his home. Hyde's house is in Soho – an area known for crime and access to the seedier side of life.

DO IT!

1 Match these quotations with the point in the novel to which they belong. What is suggested about each location by Stevenson's choice of language?

"'A fog rolled over the city in the small hours.'" ———— The night of the Carew murder

"'The street was small and…quiet.'"

Utterson is heading to Hyde's house after the Carew murder.

"'like a district of some city in a nightmare'"

The entrance to the laboratory

"'blistered and distained'"

Jekyll thinks he is free of Hyde…but then transforms without the potion.

"'It was a fine clear January day…the frost had melted…cloudless overhead'"

The door to Jekyll's laboratory from the street

2 Annotate the extract below to show what can be **inferred** from this description of Hyde's home in Soho. Two examples have been done for you.

Cheap food for the poor, in contrast with the access to money that Hyde has, suggesting that only someone with something to hide would live here.

"…the fog lifted a little and showed him a dingy street, a gin palace, a low French eating house, a shop for the retail of penny numbers and twopenny salads, many ragged children huddled in the doorways, and many women of many different nationalities passing out, key in hand, to have a morning glass…This was the home of Henry Jekyll's favourite; of a man who was heir to a quarter of a million sterling."

A reference to cheap popular crime fiction, linking Hyde in the reader's mind with horrible crimes.

REVIEW IT!

1 Which period of history was the novel written in?

2 Lanyon says that Jekyll is 'wrong in mind'. What have they argued about?

3 Why would Stevenson's readers have understood this argument more than we may do?

4 Which religion was dominant in England at the time?

5 Which name of the devil is used to refer to Hyde in the novel?

6 How did Darwin's *On the Origin of Species* challenge the teachings of the Church?

7 Why might Victorian people want to hang on to accepted beliefs rather than have new ones?

8 Which characters represent respectability in the novel?

9 Why was reputation valuable?

10 Give two examples when Utterson is most concerned to protect Jekyll's reputation.

11 How has Stevenson's interest in psychology influenced this novel?

12 The analysis of dreams was a topic that interested Stevenson. How has he used a dream in the novel?

13 Do you think this novel shows a battle between good and evil? Explain your answer.

14 Why is there little direct description of Hyde's crimes in the novel?

15 What was the Victorian attitude to sexuality?

16 What does the word 'sin' mean?

17 Suicide was both illegal and a sin. How is it fitting that Hyde is a 'self-destroyer'?

18 Does Stevenson present London in a positive light? Explain your answer.

19 Why is friendship so important to Utterson?

20 Give two reasons why Jekyll's home has two distinct parts to it.

Language, structure and form

Language

Stevenson's language can be difficult for a modern reader. The vocabulary and tone are likely to be very different from your more familiar reading materials.

Stevenson uses a range of techniques to engage and influence the reader. We will look at some of them here. Using correct terminology for language features is important to your exam essays, but your personal response to the language is key.

DEFINE IT!

euphemism – an indirect or polite word or phrase used to be less harsh or offensive than a realistic word or expression

vicarious – experiencing the feelings or actions of an event as if you were the person taking part in it, although you are not

The unsaid

Stevenson leaves much unsaid because he could not write explicitly in his time – explicit description of gory or sexual crimes would have been considered indecent and unpublishable in materials for a middle-class readership.

Jekyll indirectly describes the misbehaviours of his early life as 'irregularities'. We can only guess at what this euphemism means but both homosexuality (illegal in England until 1967) and sex outside of marriage would have been condemned at the time. Later, he refers to the 'sins' carried out as Hyde, but the specifics are left unsaid.

> "The pleasures which I made haste to seek in my disguise were, as I have said, undignified; I would scarce use a harsher term. But in the hands of Edward Hyde, they soon began to turn toward the monstrous. When I would come back from these excursions, I was
> 5 often plunged into a kind of wonder at my vicarious depravity."

DO IT!

1 'Undignified' becomes 'monstrous', which then becomes 'depravity': identify the pattern in the choice of words Stevenson uses to refer to the 'misbehaviours' in the extract. How does the choice of language used to describe Jekyll's pleasures echo what is happening to him?

2 Is the word 'excursions' a euphemism? Explain your opinion.

Religious imagery

Christianity was at the core of thinking and language. The Victorian reader would have been educated with Bible stories, was likely to attend church on Sundays and to have read the Bible or religious books. Victorian readers would have had a very visual imagination of hell and the devil. They would *believe* in hell as real whereas today we may think of it as a metaphor. Many references to Hyde include religious imagery: 'My devil', 'spirit of hell' 'child of hell'.

Metaphor and simile

You will need to explore how Stevenson's language makes you think and feel; identify why it has these effects on you and explain those ideas to the reader of your essay. You could follow this method:

1 Identify the subject of the comparison.

2 Identify the metaphor or simile.

3 What does the metaphor or simile transfer to the subject?

For example:

NAILIT

Using correct terminology for language features is important to your exam answers, but your personal response to the language is key.

Quotation	" I would leap…into the possession of a fancy brimming with images of terror, a soul boiling with causeless hatreds, and a body that seemed not strong enough to contain the raging energies of life. "
1	Jekyll's description of the terror of being Hyde.
2	The metaphor compares the terror of being Hyde to being filled with a liquid.
3	The liquid (and, therefore, the terror of being Hyde) is 'brimming…

DOIT!

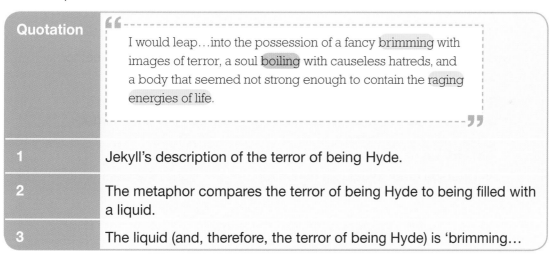

Try out the method above to explain how the simile and metaphor below add to the reader's understanding of the moment.

Quotation	Analysis
" whatever he had done, Edward Hyde would pass away like the stain of breath upon a mirror; and there in his stead…would be Henry Jekyll. "	Why has Stevenson chosen this particular simile to describe the transition from Hyde to Jekyll?
" insurgent horror was knit to him closer than a wife, closer than an eye; lay caged in his flesh, where he heard it mutter and felt it struggle to be born "	Why has Stevenson chosen each of these metaphors to describe Jekyll's attitude to Hyde?

Pathetic fallacy

Stevenson describes the weather before key moments to create a mood for the scene and sometimes to echo the emotions of the characters.

> A great chocolate-coloured pall lowered over heaven, but the wind was continually charging and routing these embattled vapours…

The fog is personified.

The wind is personified.

Extract 1

Utterson journeys to Hyde's house after Carew's murder:

Personifications of wind and fog create a visual image of the weather at war with itself.

Stevenson uses pathetic fallacy so that nature reflects Utterson's world as it has become more chaotic with the event of the murder.

Extract 2

As Utterson goes to Jekyll's house for 'the last night', the weather is again described.

> …a pale moon, lying on her back as though the wind had tilted her…[the wind] seemed to have swept the streets unusually bare of passengers…there was borne in upon his mind a crushing anticipation of calamity.

DEFINE IT!

borne in – pressing in

calamity – disaster

passengers – people

DO IT!

Follow the example above:

1 Highlight the examples of personification in extract 2.

2 Explain how the extract uses pathetic fallacy to echo Utterson's emotions.

Repetition and listing

Stevenson often uses repetition and lists within his sentences. (The repetition of ideas may use different words, but they are very similar in meaning, reinforcing the point.)

When Lanyon is looking at Hyde in his study, Stevenson uses lists to convey the experience. The lists operate in different ways, both increasing the intensity of feeling and conveying a variety of points.

Quotation	" …there was something abnormal and misbegotten… something seizing, surprising and revolting…there was added a curiosity as to his origin, his life, his fortune and status in the world. "
Identify device	Repetition restates a similar point. A list uses words to increase the intensity of feeling. A list covers a variety of points.
Why is it used?	It emphasises Hyde's deformity. This shows how the feelings grew and changed within Lanyon. This one prompts the reader to think about the stages of Hyde's development, as Lanyon is doing.

At the moment of Jekyll's transformation:

" He put the glass to his lips, and drank at one gulp. A cry followed; he reeled, staggered clutched at the table and held on, staring with injected eyes, gasping with open mouth… "

Identify the lists used here and explain *why* they are used.

Structure

Identifying how a novel is structured is a little like finding out how it is 'built'. Imagine taking apart a watch and finding how all the cogs and gears interact to make the watch work. A novel will have a variety of elements that interact to create a successful narrative. The author has chosen when and how to use these elements.

Time

We are given the sense of time progressing. It grounds the tale in a recognisable reality which is important when other elements seem fantastical.

The narrative is non-linear. It begins by following a chronology but the second and third parts go back in time to explain events from the perspectives of Dr Lanyon and Jekyll. The reader is led astray during Utterson's narration (by his incorrect judgements), and is led towards 'The Last Night' as the climax of the novel. However, although it seems to be the conclusion of the action, there is no explanation of where Jekyll – alive or dead – may be. Like Utterson, the reader then discovers, in **real time**, the accounts of Lanyon and Jekyll to draw their own conclusions about the 'Case'.

First and third person

Robert Louis Stevenson is the primary narrator of *The Strange Case of Dr Jekyll and Mr Hyde*. He narrates in the third person (which means that he is not a character in the novel) and so can view events from a more distanced perspective. However, he also allows his characters, Dr Jekyll and Dr Lanyon to narrate their own parts of the novel. This is known as first person narration (and uses the perspective of 'I') because they are narrating from their own perspective. It is used to engage the reader more closely with that character.

Evaluate the difference between use of first person and third person narration in the extracts using this table:

	Extract 1 or 2?	Explain your opinion
Which narration feels more intimate to the reader?		
Which narration gives a direct account of events?		
Which narration offers insight into the character's state of mind?		

Extract 1

"
Mr Utterson the lawyer was a man of a rugged countenance that was never lighted by a smile; cold, scanty and embarrassed in discourse; backward in sentiment; lean, long, dusty, dreary and yet somehow lovable. At friendly meetings, and when the wine was to his taste, something eminently human beaconed from his eye; something indeed which never found its way into his talk, but which spoke not only in these silent
5 symbols of the after-dinner face, but more often and loudly in the acts of his life.
"

Extract 2

"
Half an hour from now, when I shall again and forever reindue that hated personality, I know how I shall sit shuddering and weeping in my chair, or continue, with the most strained and fearstruck ecstasy of listening, to pace up and down this room (my last earthly refuge) and give ear to every sound of menace. Will Hyde die upon the scaffold? or will he find courage to release himself at the last moment? God knows;
5 I am careless; this is my true hour of death, and what is to follow concerns another than myself. Here then, as I lay down the pen and proceed to seal up my confession, I bring the life of that unhappy Henry Jekyll to an end.
"

Letters

When this novel was written, letters were the main form of written communication. They would have been transported longer distances by train and delivered on foot. Wealthier people sent their servants with important letters. Stevenson uses letters as a **structural device** to control events and to give the reader information.

Point in the plot	Effect of the letter
At the time of his murder, Carew was carrying a letter to Utterson.	This allows Utterson to be involved in the murder investigation.
After the murder, Jekyll shows Utterson a letter from Hyde but Poole says no messengers had visited the house.	This creates some doubt about the honesty of Jekyll.
When Utterson shows the letter to his clerk, he sees the handwriting is the same as Dr Jekyll's.	Again, clues are laid for Utterson and for the reader.
Utterson writes a letter to Jekyll. Jekyll replies with a confessional and puzzling letter.	Jekyll's mental instability is shown through his writing style.
After Lanyon dies, Utterson receives a letter from Lanyon that is not to be opened unless Jekyll is dead.	The sealed package increases the mystery.
Poole describes increasingly desperate and demanding letters to various chemists asking for the ingredients to make the potion.	The repeated sending of letters recreates the reality of the time and conveys the desperation felt by Jekyll.
Lanyon's narrative includes the letter from Jekyll which asks for his help.	Again, the letter demonstrates Jekyll's instability and desperation for the potion.
'Henry Jekyll's Full Statement of the Case' (Chapter 10)'	The whole chapter is a confessional letter in first person. This creates an intimacy with the reader.

Extract 1

Poole felt in his pocket and handed out a crumpled note, which the lawyer, bending nearer to the candle, carefully examined. Its contents ran thus: "Dr Jekyll presents his compliments to Messrs. Maw. He assures them that their last sample is impure and quite useless for his present purpose. In the year 18--,
5 Dr J. purchased a somewhat large quantity from Messrs. M. He now begs them to search with most sedulous care, and should any of the same quality be left, forward it to him at once. Expense is no consideration. The importance of this to Dr J. can hardly be exaggerated." So far the letter had run composedly enough, but here with a sudden splutter of the pen, the writer's emotion had broken loose.
10 "For God's sake," he added, "find me some of the old."
"This is a strange note," said Mr Utterson; and then sharply, "How do you come to have it open?"

> What clue does the letter provide about Jekyll's problems with the potion?

> How does the language of the letter reveal Jekyll's state of mind?

> What does Utterson's comment show about the relationship between master and servant in the Victorian context?

Form: the title

In the title –*The Strange Case of Dr Jekyll and Mr Hyde* – the reference to a 'case' leads the reader to expect a legal or scientific document to follow. However, Stevenson follows a different format of three parts:

Third person narration (Chapters 1–8)	'Dr Lanyon's Narrative' – in the first person (Chapter 9)	'Henry Jekyll's Full Statement of the Case' – in the first person (Chapter 10)
Stevenson, as the author, narrates the story. However, the perspective upon events is often that of Mr Utterson. Alongside this, recounts from the perspectives of other characters appear: Mr Enfield tells of the incident with the child; the account of Carew's murder is told using the language and attitudes of the maid who witnessed it; Poole gives an extended account of Jekyll's behaviour leading up to the last night. (This variation of styles enables Stevenson to increase tension without using Utterson's perspective; thus, Utterson remains grounded and relatively calm in the reader's eyes but actions have become intensified through the words of others.) Dialogues allow other characters to have a voice and vary perspective or interest for the reader. For example, Utterson's conversations with Hyde, Jekyll, the police officer and Lanyon.	Lanyon is first established as a trusted character through his association with Utterson.  He then narrates, after the climax of the plot, through his written account of events. He knows he is dying so has little reason to be unreliable. His account includes high drama but we are likely to trust him as a man of good sense. This text also includes a copy of a letter from Jekyll to Lanyon asking for help in getting the necessary powders, phial and notes. This letter sounds full of panic and desperation.	This is the last and longest chapter in the novel. Henry Jekyll had written it shortly before his death.  It includes information about his family and youth which are not mentioned in the rest of the novel. It explains his reasons for attempting and continuing with the experiments in personality separation. It is calmer and more logical than the letter included in Lanyon's narrative and so appears more credible. It is in the form of a confession. This was a popular form of narration in the Victorian era – both real and fictional.
The reader must think like a detective, looking for clues to an unspecified puzzle.	The reader looks for confirmation or correction of his or her deductions from the previous chapters.	The reader has a continuous explanation of previous events.

Detection and discovery

Stevenson positions the Victorian reader in a 'detective role' by uncovering some parts of the truth while keeping others hidden for later discovery. Due to the fame of the story, it can be difficult for today's readers to appreciate Stevenson's careful reveal of details throughout the novel.

REVIEW IT!

1 Find an example of a simile used to describe Hyde.

2 Find an example of personification used to describe the weather.

3 What is the name of the technique when nature seems to share human emotions?

4 Find an example of religious imagery.

5 What name for the devil is frequently used?

6 Why was religious imagery so effective on Stevenson's Victorian readership?

7 Why do we not learn in detail of Hyde's crimes?

8 "
> A moment before I had been safe of all men's respect, wealthy, beloved…and now I was the common quarry of mankind, hunted, houseless, a known murderer, thrall to the gallows.
"

Identify the lists in this quotation.

9 Why has Stevenson used lists here?

10 When Poole and Utterson are preparing to break into the laboratory:

"
> The scud had banked over the moon, and it was now quite dark. The wind, which only broke in puffs and draughts into that deep well of building, tossed the light of the candle to and fro about their steps…
"

Explain how this atmosphere suits what is about to happen.

11 How many 'official' narrators are there in the novel? Name them.

12 From whose perspective is much of the novel seen? Why has Stevenson chosen this perspective?

13 Why does Stevenson refer to time so regularly?

14 How did communication in Victorian times differ from now?

15 Give two examples of letters being used in the plot.

16 How does handwriting play a role in the plot?

17 What do we learn of Jekyll's state of mind from his first letter to Utterson?

18 What do we learn of Jekyll's state of mind from his note to the chemist?

19 What do we learn of Jekyll's state of mind from his letter to Lanyon?

20 Why is the final chapter in Jekyll's own voice?

Doing well in your AQA exam

- In your AQA exam the extract will come before the question
- **Read the question before you read the extract** so that you read the extract with the question focus in mind.
- Read the question carefully and understand it. Make sure you stay relevant to the question.

Understanding the question

Make sure you understand the exam question so that you do not include irrelevant material in your answer. Explore the extract *in relation to the question* rather than simply in terms of anything that grabs your attention.

The question below has been annotated by a student so that they fully understand it.

> When do we feel sympathetic towards Jekyll (events; relationships)? Sympathy from a Victorian/modern reader – same or different?

> How far – I can agree and/or disagree (on one/the other hand).

AQA exam-style question

- Starting with this extract, explore how far Stevenson presents Jekyll as worthy of sympathy in the novel.

> How does he want me to feel about him?

Write about:

- how Stevenson presents Jekyll in this extract
- how Stevenson presents Jekyll in the novel as a whole.

This student has studied the question carefully and realised that:

- the focus is on Jekyll as a sympathetic figure
- 'how far' means the student can agree and/or disagree or a bit of both
- 'sympathy' can be considered from both a modern and a Victorian view
- our feelings about Jekyll have been controlled by Stevenson.

'Pinning the question down' like this – making sure it is fully understood – has allowed the student to then pick out of the extract some useful evidence to support the answer.

Choose a question from earlier in this guide. 'Pin the question down' as above.

Aim to discuss two or three examples from the rest of the novel in comparison with the example from the extract for each paragraph.

Planning your answer

Once you have made sure you fully understand the question, planning an answer will be quite straightforward. Your brief plan should set out:

- your key, *relevant* ideas
- the content of each of four or five paragraphs
- the order of the paragraphs.

Here is the same student's plan for their answer to the exam question on page 84:

Paragraph	Content		Timing plan
1	Intro - use the question preparation to establish focus of answer		9.40
2	Explore extract - evidence of reader's sympathy		9.43
3	Jekyll's presentation as likeable character	Refer back to extract.	9.58
4	Pity - mental/physical pain		10.06
5	Judgement of failings - from other characters/contemporary reader/modern reader	Refer back to question focus. Question how far 'sympathy' is generated.	10.14
6	Conclusion - brief return to question		10.22

Sticking to the plan

Note how this student has jotted down time points when they should move on to the next section of their answer. That way they make sure they do not get stuck on one point and fail to cover the question focus in enough breadth.

Planning to meet the mark scheme

The plan above suggests that the student has thought carefully about the task in the question, that they are familiar with the mark scheme for their AQA 19th-century novel question and are planning to cover its requirements. (See the summary mark scheme on page 86.)

Assessment objective (AO)	What the plan promises
AO1 Read, understand and respond 12 marks	Understanding of a number of ideas relevant to the main question focus – likeability, pity for suffering, judgement of failings Some personal interpretations to be included.
AO2 Language, form and structure 12 marks	Exploring the extract will ensure close engagement with Stevenson's language and structure.
AO3 Contexts 6 marks	Jekyll's rebellion against accepted beliefs of the time. Consideration of how a modern audience may view him – how might we feel about him?

NAILIT!

In your AQA exam, spend 10–15 minutes on understanding the question and planning your answer. There are no marks for using lots of words. Instead, you should aim to write enough *good, useful* words. Aim for four or five well-planned paragraphs (plus an introduction and conclusion if necessary).

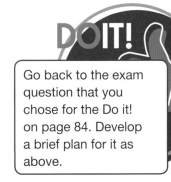

DOIT!

Go back to the exam question that you chose for the Do it! on page 84. Develop a brief plan for it as above.

What your AQA examiner is looking for

Your AQA examiner will mark your answer according to a mark scheme based on three assessment objectives (AOs). The AOs focus on specific knowledge, understanding and skills. Together, they are worth 30 marks, so it is important to understand what the examiner is looking out for.

Mark scheme

Your AQA examiner will mark your answers in 'bands'. These bands roughly equate as follows:

- band 6 approx. grades 8 and 9
- band 5 approx. grades 6 and 7
- band 4 approx. grades 5 and 6
- band 3 approx. grades 3 and 4
- band 2 approx. grades 1 and 2.

Most importantly, the improvement descriptors below – based on the AQA mark scheme – will help you understand how to improve your answers and gain more marks. The maximum number of marks for each AO is shown.

Assessment objective (AO)		Improvement descriptors				
		Band 2 Your answer…	**Band 3** Your answer…	**Band 4** Your answer…	**Band 5** Your answer…	**Band 6** Your answer…
AO1 12 marks	**Read, understand and respond**	is relevant and backs up ideas with references to the novel	sometimes explains the novel in relation to the question	clearly explains the novel in relation to the question	thoughtfully explains the novel in relation to the question	critically explores the novel in relation to the question
	Use evidence	makes some comments about these references	refers to details in the novel to back up points	carefully chooses close references to the novel to back up points	thoughtfully builds appropriate references into points	chooses precise details from the novel to make points convincing
AO2 12 marks	**Language, form and structure**	mentions some of Stevenson's methods.	comments on some of Stevenson's methods, and their effects	clearly explains Stevenson's key methods, and their effects	thoughtfully explores Stevenson's methods, and their effects	analyses Stevenson's methods, and how these influence the reader
	Subject terminology	uses some subject terminology	uses some relevant terminology	helpfully uses varied, relevant terminology	makes thoughtful use of relevant terminology	chooses subject terminology to make points precise and convincing
AO3 6 marks	**Contexts**	makes some simple inferences about contexts.	infers Stevenson's point of view and the significance of contexts.	shows a clear appreciation of Stevenson's point of view and the significance of contexts.	explores Stevenson's point of view and the significance of relevant contexts.	makes perceptive and revealing links between the play and relevant contexts.

AO1 Read, understand and respond/Use evidence

Make sure you read and answer the question carefully and thoughtfully. The examiner will be looking for evidence that you have answered the question. Do not make the mistake of going into the exam with an answer in mind: you must concentrate on the aspect that the question focuses on. Knowing the novel well will give you the confidence to do that.

Using evidence means supporting your ideas with references to the novel. They can be indirect references – brief mentions of an event or what a character says or does – or direct references – quotations. Choose and use evidence carefully so that it really does support a point you are making. Quotations should be as short as possible, and the very best ones are often neatly built into your writing.

AO2 Language, form and structure/Subject terminology

Remember that *The Strange Case of Dr Jekyll and Mr Hyde* is not real life. It is a novel that Stevenson has *created* to entertain and influence the reader. The language and other methods he uses have been chosen carefully for effect. Good answers will not just point out good words Stevenson has used: they will explore the author's intent and likely effects of those word choices on the reader.

Subject terminology is about choosing your words carefully, using the right words and avoiding vague expressions. It is also about using terminology *helpfully*. For example, here are two different uses of subject terminology, the first much more useful than the second:

Student answer A

When Jekyll writes of his experience of taking the potion for the first time, he uses the metaphor of 'an angel or a fiend' to refer to the possible outcomes. The connotations of 'angel' as blessed by God, doing His good work within the world link it with Jekyll's ideal self; the 'fiend' implies a link to Satan, in opposition to God and taking people from the path of righteousness. This language would be particularly powerful and familiar to a Victorian Christian readership who would have been highly aware of the religious associations of these opposites.

Student answer B

'Angel or a fiend' is a good metaphor to describe Jekyll's options.

Student B identifies a language feature. Student A **evaluates** the language chosen in relation to its context and potential effect on the reader.

AO3 Contexts

Context is important when it helps the audience to understand and interpret the meaning and ideas within the novel. Consider how might:

- the society Stevenson lived in have influenced his ideas and attitudes?

- the society *you* live in have influenced how *you* respond to ideas and attitudes in the novel?

- knowledge of the whole novel enrich your understanding of the extract?

The best answers will include contextual information that is directly relevant to the *question*, not just the novel. See pages 68–72 for more information and guidance on how to make the most of contexts in your writing.

NAILIT!

To boost your marks when answering questions, do the following:

- Know the novel well. Read it and study it.

- Don't go into the exam with ready-prepared answers.

- Read the question and make sure you answer it thoughtfully.

- Choose details in the novel that will support your points.

- Don't treat the novel and its characters as though they are real. Instead ask why Stevenson has chosen to create a particular dialogue or event. What effect is he trying to achieve?

NAILIT!

Introductions and conclusions need to be useful or they simply waste time. Your opening:

- should be short and relevant
- could introduce a particular angle on the question, or interpretation
- could answer the question directly (leaving the rest of the answer to provide supporting detail).

DOIT!

Student A's is the better introduction. Explain why, using the success criteria on page 86.

Writing your answer

Getting started

Here are the openings of two students' answers to the question on page 84 about how far Jekyll is worthy of sympathy in *The Strange Case of Dr Jekyll and Mr Hyde*:

Student answer A

Although Jekyll is the origin and creator of the evil Hyde, it is easy to forget this for much of the novel because we do not actually know this until the last chapters. Throughout the novel, we are presented with a man who is well-liked by his friends, who has misjudged Hyde and appears to be suffering some kind of mental torment...even though we may be suspicious of him. In his full statement in Chapter 10, we are in a position to judge him and may be more critical. Stevenson has designed his novel so that the reader has to view Jekyll from different perspectives and so our sympathy may vary throughout.

Student answer B

I am going to write about how far I agree that Jekyll is worthy of sympathy. Clearly, he did bad things because he created Hyde and Hyde went on to kill people. This is Jekyll's fault because he created him. However, he also suffers a lot too. I am going to write about when he seems to be good and when he is bad and make a judgement.

The extract

You do not need to write about the extract and *then* about the rest of the novel. If you feel confident about it, then compare the extract with other parts of the novel throughout your answer. However, a safer approach – just to make sure you do give the extract enough attention – is to begin with the extract and then make connections with other parts of the novel in the following paragraphs. This is the approach suggested in the plan you have already looked at.

Here is part of that student's writing about the extract. Note the way they use the extract to closely examine relevant details of Stevenson's language choices. An examiner has made some comments in the margin.

We may pity Jekyll for the intensity of his mental breakdown. Stevenson clearly conveys this when he lists the effects of 'sits shuddering, weeping...most strained...fear-struck'. By placing all the effects so closely together, we get the sense of Jekyll's decline each time another image is added to our imaginations. We appreciate his fear more fully when he uses religious imagery to say that the room is his 'last earthly refuge'. 'Earthly' implies that he is also thinking of the opposite – heaven or hell. A Victorian reader would have had a very clear and real image in their heads of what hell would be like and would be able to understand Jekyll's torment at this prospect.

Effect explored

Useful terminology.

Effect of words is identified.

Paragraph topics

The rest of your paragraphs should each deal with a sub-topic of the main focus of the question. Here, the question focuses on Jekyll as worthy of sympathy. The student's plan suggests that the next three paragraph topics will be: his likeability, then pity, then of his failings. Each of the paragraphs will help the student to address the 'how far' aspect of the question: in other words, the student can explore whether Jekyll is worthy of sympathy at a variety of points throughout the novel and in different contexts.

Below you will see how – in this beginning of the 'pity' paragraph – the same student makes references back to both the extract and the question so as to stay sharply relevant. The references to the question are underlined to point them out.

In his full statement, Jekyll may be pitied for both his physical and mental suffering. Described here as the 'throes of change,' we are again reminded that the transformation itself is painful, as it appeared when he 'reeled, staggered, clutched' in front of Lanyon. He is arriving at 'the last of the old powders' which recalls his desperate seeking for the drugs in his letters to the chemist. A Victorian audience would have held little sympathy with that demonstration of lack of control, 'for God's sake', but a modern reader who is likely to be better informed about addictions may have some pity for his addict-like slavery to a substance.

> Using evidence:
> This student uses direct evidence from the extract in the form of a quotation but uses indirect evidence when referring to another part of the text. Direct and indirect evidence from the novel as a whole are also used. Both forms of evidence are valid, but do quote from the extract at least – if only to show you can handle quotations.

Ending your answer

If you write a conclusion, make it useful: don't simply repeat what you have already said. The answer we have been looking at ends with this summary:

Across the novel, Jekyll deserves sympathy for his weaknesses and suffering, and also his desire to be ahead of his time and reject restrictive beliefs about science, which force his experiments to be done in isolation. However, the side of himself that is unleashed is guilty of causing suffering to others, and it is still his own self, it is part of who he is and so Hyde's actions are actually Jekyll's own. On balance, like anyone, he is worthy of both sympathy and criticism - though a Victorian audience would probably give him a harsher judgement than a modern one.

DO IT!

Use the preparation and planning you did for your chosen exam question (see page 84) to write a full answer.

STRETCH IT!

Develop a range of evaluative vocabulary to enable you to pinpoint the writer's intention. Use words like: 'condemns', 'criticises', 'exposes', 'ridicules', 'subverts', 'questions'.

Going for the top grades

Of course you will always try to write the best answer possible, but if you are aiming for the top grades then it is vital to be clear about what examiners will be looking out for. The best answers will tend to:

• show a clear understanding of both the novel *and* the exam question • show insight into the novel and the question focus • explore the novel in relation to the focus of the question • choose and use evidence precisely and wisely	**AO1**
• analyse Stevenson's methods and their effect on the reader • use relevant, helpful subject terminology	**AO2**
• explore aspects of context that are relevant to the novel and the question.	**AO3**

A great answer **will not** waste words or use evidence for its own sake.

A great answer **will** show that you are engaging directly and thoughtfully with the novel, not just scribbling down everything you have been told about it.

The best answers will be RIPE with ideas and engagement:

R	Relevant	Stay strictly relevant to the question.
I	Insightful	Develop relevant insights into the novel, its characters, and themes.
P	Precise	Choose and use evidence precisely so that it strengthens your points.
E	Exploratory	Explore relevant aspects of the novel, looking at it from more than one angle.

Find an essay or practice answer you have written about *The Strange Case of Dr Jekyll and Mr Hyde*. Use the advice and examples on this page to help you decide how your writing could be improved.

Below is a small part of a student's answer to the question on page 84 about how far Jekyll deserves sympathy. An examiner has made some comments in the margin.

Although Jekyll is clearly suffering, a reader's sympathy will beaffected by the judgements made about his behaviour and choices. Hyde is presented as a separate character from Jekyll and the novel focuses on how violent, 'tear it to pieces' and animalistic, 'ape-like spite' Hyde is; he is described in similar waysat the murder of Carew and when he appears to Lanyon. Jekyll is distressed by and fears Hyde so the reader may have some sympathy for his suffering. However, the reader is aware that Hyde and Jekyll are one and the same, and that Jekyll created him. This may reduce a reader's sympathy because Jekyll consciously upset the natural order with his experiment - it is his own fault. The Victorian reader could have considered that he is paying the price for his arrogance in 'playing God'. The novel aimed to shock its readers by dealing with topics that they were frightened by - such as science challenging religious beliefs - and seeing Jekyll suffer may have pleased some rather than make them feel sympathetic to him.

Clear and **nuanced** point.

Precise choice of evidence.

Precise evidence neatly integrated into argument.

Ironies of Jekyll's position explored here.

Original insight based on context.

Good return to question focus to maintain relevance.

REVIEW IT!

1 What should you do before you read the extract from the novel?

2 Why should you do that before reading the extract?

3 How long should you spend on understanding the question and planning the answer?

4 What three things should be covered in your plan?

5 Why is it helpful to build timings into your plan?

6 How many paragraphs is a good number to plan for?

7 Why is it useful to know the mark scheme?

8 Your friend has told you that they are going to learn an essay that they wrote in the mock exams as their revision. What would you say?

9 Do you have to write about the extract before writing about the rest of the novel?

10 What should each paragraph of your answer be about?

11 Must you quote from the extract?

12 What is meant by 'evidence'?

13 What should be the focus of your revision in the final month?

14 It is vital that your answer is relevant. Relevant to what?

15 What four ideas should be kept in mind when trying to write a top grade answer?

16 Should you write an introduction to your essay?

17 What is the function of an introduction?

18 What is the function of a conclusion?

19 Why is this a bad conclusion to an answer?

> So that is what I think - Jekyll is a weak man. I think I've made it clear why.

20 Why is this a better conclusion?

> So, in the end it probably depends on your view of Jekyll. You could admire his inventiveness in challenging the accepted views of his time, or you might criticise his selfishness in doing what he wants without regard for the consequences. You could admire his inventiveness or criticise his vanity.

NAIL IT!

In the month leading up to the exam, all your revision should be based on planning and writing answers to exam questions. You will find plenty of AQA exam-style questions in this *Study Guide*.

AQA exam-style questions

On these pages you will find two practice questions for *The Strange Case of Dr Jekyll and Mr Hyde*. In the exam you will only get one question: you will not have a choice of questions. Self-assessment guidance is provided on the app/online.

PRACTICE QUESTION 1

Read the following extract from the first chapter of *The Strange Case of Dr Jekyll and Mr Hyde* and then answer the question that follows.

At this point in the novel, Mr Enfield is describing how he first met Mr Hyde.

> He was perfectly cool and made no resistance, but gave me one look, so ugly that it brought out the sweat on me like running. The people who had turned out were the girl's own family; and pretty soon, the doctor, for whom she had been sent, put in his appearance. Well, the child was not much the worse,
> 5 more frightened, according to the Sawbones; and there you might have supposed would be an end to it. But there was one curious circumstance. I had taken a loathing to my gentleman at first sight. So had the child's family, which was only natural. But the doctor's case was what struck me. He was the usual cut and dry apothecary, of no particular age and colour, with a strong
> 10 Edinburgh accent, and about as emotional as a bagpipe. Well, sir, he was like the rest of us; every time he looked at my prisoner, I saw that Sawbones turn sick and white with desire to kill him. I knew what was in his mind, just as he knew what was in mine; and killing being out of the question, we did the next best. We told the man we could and would make such a scandal out
> 15 of this, as should make his name stink from one end of London to the other. If he had any friends or any credit, we undertook that he should lose them. And all the time, as we were pitching it in red hot, we were keeping the women off him as best we could for they were as wild as harpies. I never saw a circle of such hateful faces; and there was the man in the middle, with a kind of
> 20 black, sneering coolness – frightened too, I could see that – but carrying it off, sir, really like Satan. "If you choose to make capital out of this accident," said he, "I am naturally helpless. No gentleman but wishes to avoid a scene," says he. "Name your figure." Well, we screwed him up to a hundred pounds for the child's family; he would have clearly liked to stick out; but there was
> 25 something about the lot of us that meant mischief, and at last he struck.

Starting with this moment in the novel, explore how far Stevenson presents Hyde as evil.

Write about:
- how Stevenson presents Hyde at this moment in the novel
- how Stevenson presents Hyde in the novel as a whole.

[30 marks]

PRACTICE QUESTION 2

Read the following extract from *The Strange Case of Dr Jekyll and Mr Hyde* and then answer the question that follows.

At this point in the novel, Mr Utterson visits Dr Jekyll after the murder of Sir Danvers Carew.

…there, close up to the warmth, sat Dr Jekyll, looking deathly sick. He did not rise to meet his visitor, but held out a cold hand and bade him welcome in a changed voice.

"And now," said Mr Utterson, as soon as Poole had left them, "you have
5 heard the news?"

The doctor shuddered. "They were crying it in the square," he said. "I heard them in my dining-room."

"One word," said the lawyer. "Carew was my client, but so are you, and I want to know what I am doing. You have not been mad enough to hide
10 this fellow?"

"Utterson, I swear to God," cried the doctor, "I swear to God I will never set eyes on him again. I bind my honour to you that I am done with him in this world. It is all at an end. And indeed he does not want my help; you do not know him as I do; he is safe, he is quite safe; mark my words, he will never
15 more be heard of."

The lawyer listened gloomily; he did not like his friend's feverish manner. "You seem pretty sure of him," said he; "and for your sake, I hope you may be right. If it came to a trial, your name might appear."

"I am quite sure of him," replied Jekyll; "I have grounds for certainty that I
20 cannot share with anyone. But there is one thing on which you may advise me. I have – I have received a letter; and I am at a loss whether I should show it to the police. I should like to leave it in your hands, Utterson; you would judge wisely, I am sure; I have so great a trust in you."

"You fear, I suppose, that it might lead to his detection?" asked the lawyer.
25 "No," said the other. "I cannot say that I care what becomes of Hyde; I am quite done with him. I was thinking of my own character, which this hateful business has rather exposed."

Starting with this conversation, explore how Stevenson presents the theme of reputation in the novel.

Write about:
• how Stevenson presents the value of a good reputation in this extract
• how Stevenson presents the value of a good reputation in the novel as a whole.

[30 marks]

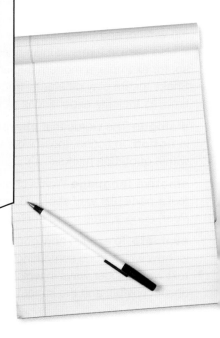

Glossary

abstract noun A noun meaning an idea or state instead of a concrete object (or example: *truth*, *happiness*).

argument A point of view that is explained and defended. An argument in a text might be a writer's exploration of both sides of a point of view.

character A person in a play or story: a person created by the writer.

characterisation How a character has been written by the author; how the author presents the character so that we see them in a particular way.

colloquial language Informal language that is normally used in speech rather than writing (for example: *They're out* rather than *They are not at home*; *yeah* rather than *yes*).

colloquial metaphor A metaphor using informal language (for example: It *was a tough nut to crack*). See **colloquial language** and **metaphor**.

connotation The implied meaning of a word of phrase. See **implicit**. For example, the word *mob* means a large group of people, but it *connotes* violence. If someone *dashes* down the road, we know that they are moving quickly, but that choice of word also connotes urgency. A connotation is sometimes called a *nuance*.

context The context of a poem, play, novel or story is the set of conditions in which it was written. These might include: the writer's life; society, habits and beliefs at the time they wrote; an event that influenced the writing; and the genre of the writing. The context is also seen in terms of influences on the reader, so, for example, a modern audience would see a Shakespeare play differently from audiences in his own time, as their life experiences would be different.

dialogue The words that **characters** say in plays or in **fiction**. In fiction, these words are usually shown within quotation marks ('…').

emotive language Words chosen to make a reader feel a particular way about something (for example: *Poor, hungry, little mites* or *Great, hulking bullies*).

evaluate To explain how good (or bad) something is: how well it does something. When we evaluate a text we consider ways in which it is successful (or unsuccessful), and the impact it has on us.

euphemism An indirect or polite word or phrase used intentionally to be less harsh or offensive than a realistic word or expression (for example: *alternative facts* = lies; *kicked the bucket* = died).

evidence Details or clues that support a point of view. A quotation can be a form of evidence in which a few words are copied from a text to support a point of view.

explicit Explicit information is clearly stated; it's on the surface of a text and should be obvious.

fiction Novels or stories made up by an author.

foreshadowing A clue or a warning about a future event.

Gothic literature A genre of literature and film that combines fiction and horror, death, and at times romance. See **fiction**.

hiatus A pause in which nothing happens or is said.

hyperbole Exaggerated statements for rhetorical effect.

hypocrisy When people or **characters** claim to have higher standards of behaviour or beliefs than is actually the case.

imagery The 'pictures' a writer puts into the reader's mind. **Similes** and **metaphors** are particular forms of imagery. We also talk about violent, graphic or religious imagery, and so on.

implicit (imply) Implicit information is only suggested (or implied), it is not stated directly; we have to **infer** to understand it. The opposite of **explicit**.

infer (inference) To 'read between the lines'; to work out meaning from clues in the text. See **implicit**. When we infer, we are making an inference.

interpret To work out meaning, using clues and **evidence**. The same piece of writing can be interpreted in different ways, but evidence has to support interpretations.

ironic Happening in a way contrary to what is expected, and typically causing some amusement because of this.

language (choices) The words and the style that a writer chooses in order to have an effect on a reader.

metaphor A comparison of one thing to another without the use of like or as (for example: His face *was a thunder cloud*. The boy *was an angry bear*).

naturalistic Creating an impression of real life.

nuance Implied meaning. See **connotation**.

pathetic fallacy A term to describe the giving of human emotion and behaviour to nature, for example: water, landscape. It can be used to imply the emotions of a **character**.

perspective Another term for viewpoint. Our perspective is how we 'see' things.

plot The plot of a literary text is the *story* – the narrative – or an interrelated series of events as described by the author.

quotation A word, phrase, sentence or passage copied from a text, usually used to support an **argument** or point of view. A quotation should be surrounded by quotation marks ('…'). It is usually wise to make quotations as short as possible, sometimes just one well-chosen word is enough.

real time The actual time during which a series of events occur.

rhetorical device A use of language to elicit an emotional response from the reader/audience.

setting The setting is the *time and place* in which a story or play takes place. The setting could also include the social and political circumstances (or **context**) of the action.

simile Comparing two things using either the word *like* or *as* (for example: The boy was *like an angry bear*. His running *was as loud as thunder*. Her face was *as yellow as custard*).

structural device A method a writer uses to give their writing shape and create effects. Structural devices include: a story arc with a beginning, middle and end; flashback; dual narrative (gives two sides of a story with alternating viewpoints) or circular narrative (the last line of a piece takes you back to the beginning of it). See **structural feature**.

structural feature A feature used by a writer to give their writing shape and coherence. These are the features that hold writing together. Structural features include: **tone**, style, repetitions, extended images, shifts of focus, voice and viewpoint, openings and closings, sequencing of ideas, links between paragraphs and sentences.

structure How a text is organised and held together: all those things that shape a text and make it coherent.

style Writing styles can vary between writers, or writers may use different styles at different times (for example: they might sometimes write informally with energy, while in other texts they might write formally, creating a style that gives them an air of authority). Style and **tone** are closely related.

subject terminology The technical words that are used for a particular subject. All the words in this glossary are subject terminology for English literature.

theme A theme is a central idea in a text. Common themes in novels, play scripts, film scripts, poems and other literary texts include: loyalty, love, race, betrayal, poverty, good versus evil, and so on.

tone The mood of a text, or the attitude of the author or narrator towards the topic. Tones can be mocking, affectionate, polite, authoritative, and so on.

vocabulary The words a writer chooses to use. They might use a particular sort of vocabulary (for example: formal, simple or shocking).

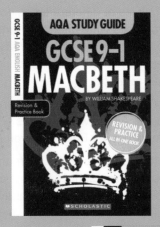
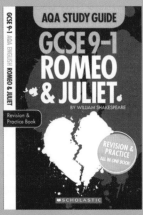
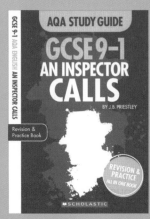
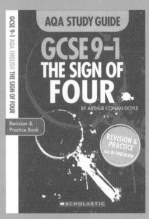

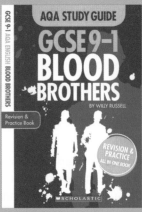